from borshch *to* blinis

from borshch *to* blinis

GREAT TRADITIONAL COOKING
FROM RUSSIA AND POLAND

Contributing Editor LESLEY CHAMBERLAIN
Author CATHERINE ATKINSON

southwater

This edition is published by Southwater

Southwater is an imprint of Anness Publishing Limited
Hermes House
88–89 Blackfriars Road
London SE1 8HA
tel. 020 7401 2077; fax 020 7633 9499

Distributed in the UK by The Manning Partnership
251–253 London Road East
Batheaston
Bath BA1 7RL
tel. 01225 852 727; fax 01225 852 852

Distributed in the USA by Anness Publishing Inc.
27 West 20th Street
Suite 504
New York
NY 10011
tel. 212 807 6739; fax 212 807 6813

Distributed in Australia by Sandstone Publishing
Unit 1, 360 Norton Street
Leichhardt
New South Wales 2040
Australia
tel. (0061) 2 9560 7888; fax (0061) 2 9560 7488

1 3 5 7 9 10 8 6 4 2

Publisher: Joanna Lorenz
Editor: Margaret Malone
Photography: Ian Garlick
Styling: Shannon Beare
Food for Photography: Clare Lewis, assisted by Sascha Brodie
Illustrators: Angela Wood (artworks) and David Cook (map)
Production Controller: Don Campaniello
Picture Credits: p 7 The Stock Market

Previously published as part of a larger compendium,
The Practical Encyclopedia of East European Cooking

CONTENTS

INTRODUCTION

The region occupied by Russia, Poland and the Ukraine has a tradition of peasant cooking, defined by the tart flavours of sourdough rye bread, pickles and sauerkraut, and complemented by mushrooms, herring, onion and sausage. These simple foods reflect what the often poor soil yielded in the harsh climate, and what could be preserved by traditional means (in salt or vinegar or by drying) for year-round use. Hardy root and vegetable crops, a variety of grains, the flavours of garlic, mustard and horseradish, and sour dairy products, such as yogurt and buttermilk (the Russian *kefir),* were the region's staples. Cabbage and cucumbers, fresh or pickled, were the primary sources of vitamin C in what, for centuries, was a highly restricted diet.

RELIGIOUS INFLUENCES

In Russia and those parts of the Ukraine where the Russian Orthodox Church determined popular eating habits, at least until the beginning of the 20th century, the Church made a virtue out of economic necessity. It divided foods into two groups. For over half the days of the year only Lenten fare was allowed: vegetables, fish and mushrooms. Milk, eggs and meat were permitted on the remaining days.

The result of this intervention was a good number of simple, versatile recipes. A full meal might consist of a cabbage soup with a grain porridge called *kasha.* Meat, if available, would be cooked in the soup but served separately afterwards. On full fast days, mushrooms could be substituted for meat to give the soup flavour and perhaps to fill little pies or *pirozhki* to eat alongside it.

Buckwheat pancakes and soured cream, typical of the meat-free Carnival Week, now rank among the best-liked Russian dishes in the world. Russian Easter food, centred on roast suckling pig basted in soured cream and a cake, *kulich,* served with a sweet cream cheese, is a splendidly rich contrast with the simpler Lenten food that precedes it.

In Poland, there are 12 Lenten dishes – to equal the number of apostles – including a beetroot soup, herring, carp in black sauce and a mushroom dish. Christmas is an important time for the Roman Catholic Church and the elaborate Polish meal on Christmas Eve is gastronomically typical.

RECENT CHANGES

Two factors in the 19th century began to modernize the East European peasant diet. One was the industrialization that brought peasants into the towns and saw middle-class cooking influenced by cosmopolitan ideas. The other was the impact of the eating habits of the royal courts on the cuisines of both Russia and Poland, which eventually filtered down through the aristocracy to the bourgeoisie.

Left: The recipes in this book cover an area that stretches from the Baltic Sea in the north to the Caspian and Black Seas in the south. From Russia, the Baltic countries and Poland in the north, through the Ukraine and down to the edge of Turkey and the Middle East, these recipes reflect the wonderful diversity and the overall defining culinary characteristics of classic East European food.

Right: Open-air cooking on a large scale in Yakut, former USSR.

THE ROYAL COURTS

The Polish court flourished in the 16th century, when Poland's empire stretched from the Baltic to the Black Sea and the educated minority enjoyed an artistic and political culture, rich in contacts with Renaissance Europe. The Italian connection was particularly strong, due to the Italian-born Queen Bona Sforza who brought with her an entourage and ideas about cooking when she married King Sigismund in 1518. As a consequence, southern European vegetables were planted in the garden of the Royal Court at Krakow. Bona Sforza is also associated with Polish ice cream, pasta and cakes – Polish *babka* being really a first cousin to Italian *panettone*.

In the 19th century, access to French cookery books led to Polish cooking becoming richer than Russian in, for example, sauces and composite tastes. At the same time, however, the Russian upper classes also felt under constant pressure to "Frenchify" their own cooking, the court and aristocracy mainly employing French chefs to produce elaborate dishes, replete with butter and cream. Antonïn Carême, as cook to Alexander I (Tsar 1801–25), began a task that was continued by four generations of foreign chefs up to the Russian Revolution.

Generally, however, there was always opposition to this outside influence, and patriotic palates preferred the traditional breads, grains and soups. One such example is *borshch*, the famous beetroot soup, whose origin cannot be fixed within any present-day national confines. It can be served as a consommé or as a thick soup.

By contrast the Russian cold table, originally borrowed from Scandinavia during the reign of the great Westernizing Tsar, Peter I (1682-1725), has been wholly incorporated into the national cuisine as the classic first course. Comprising little open sandwich hors d'oeuvres, these *zakuski* dishes, which are washed down with ice-cold vodka, deserve their fame, especially as the jewel of the *zakuski* table is often caviare.

INGREDIENTS

VEGETABLES AND MUSHROOMS

Ridge cucumbers, with a firm texture and full flavour, are either used fresh in salads or pickled in bottles for winter. Other popular vegetables are beetroot, potato, carrots, parsnips and fresh cabbage, all of which grow well in a cold climate and can be stored all year round. Cabbage is also fermented in brine, with spices, to make the widely available sauerkraut. As for spring onions, both the white bulbs and the green tips contribute to the characteristic flavour of East European composite salads.

The romance of mushroom hunting belongs to the forests of Eastern Europe, where many varieties are found. Mushrooms are dried for use in soups and sauces, or salted or pickled for snacks with bread and vodka. They are also sautéed fresh in butter and herbs, or sauced with soured cream.

Top left, clockwise from left: pickled beetroot, sauerkraut, pickled cucumbers, dill pickles and caperberries.

Top right, clockwise: red and white cabbage, beetroot, cucumbers, mushrooms, parsnips, potatoes and carrots.

Right, from top left: Black and red lumpfish roe, salmon caviar, pike, salmon, carp and herring.

FISH

The most celebrated fish of this region belong to the sturgeon family. Of this family, both the beluga and the sevruga produce the highly prized black caviare. Freshwater salmon varieties are also very important, both for their firm flesh and for the "red" caviare so often seen on *zakuski* tables. Carp is traditional in Poland and is nowadays farmed. Herring is popular everywhere, although increasingly only the canned product is available. Pike, perch and pike-perch are the grand old river fish, yielding a firm white flesh that is suitable for pies and baked fish dishes.

DAIRY PRODUCTS

Soured cream takes the place of an oil in dressing East European salads of raw and cooked vegetables. It is the essential accompaniment to soups and pancakes and the basis for modern sauced dishes such as Beef Stroganov. It is also used in baking cakes and biscuits.

The traditional East European cheeses are made with cow's milk and are young and mild. Curd cheese is used to make savoury dips and *paskha*, the sweet Easter cream. Curd cheese can be used alone or with other ingredients to make savoury or sweet patties; it is also used to stuff pasta and pies, and forms the basis for the traditional cheesecake. *Brinza*, similar to Greek feta, is a brine cheese common all over Eastern and Central Europe, which appears in starters and pies.

MEAT DISHES

Sucking pig is a traditional Russian delicacy, as is the game bird called *ryabchik*, or hazel-hen. Plentiful use is made of beef for braising and stewing. Polish sausage is made of top-quality pork and veal, flavoured with garlic and mustard seed.

GRAINS

The Russian word *kasha* and the related words in Polish and Ukrainian denote any cooked grain. Semolina, millet, oats and buckwheat are eaten at breakfast, usually cooked in water or milk and served with butter. Buckwheat, rice, millet or barley accompany savoury dishes. Buckwheat, actually a relative of the rhubarb family rather than a grain, is cooked into *kasha* and its flour is used to make traditional Shrovetide pancakes, or *blini*. It grows prolifically in Eastern Europe, and its recognizable smoky taste is characteristic of traditional peasant cooking.

Sourdough breads from this area have a distinctive, satisfying quality, thanks to their being made with rye flour by a sour fermentation process. This produces long-lasting loaves with excellent digestive properties, ranging from straw-coloured bread to the distinctly black Russian *borodinsky*, which is made with molasses and has its crust studded with coriander seeds.

HERBS, SPICES AND OTHER FLAVOURINGS

Dill, the most common herb in Eastern and Central European cooking, adds a distinct freshness to pickles as well as to salads and cooked dishes. The feathery leaves needed for authentic cooking lose much of their taste when dried so they should always be used fresh. The pungent seeds can be used in sauerkraut dishes and stews. Parsley, of the pungent, flat leaf variety, is also widely used in soups and salads and as a garnish, while the root adds flavour to stocks and soup bases. Fresh garlic adds piquancy to soups and stews, while mustard and horseradish give bite to fish and meat dishes.

FRUIT

East Europe has a strong tradition of domestic jam-making and bottling every available fruit and vegetable, from excellent plum jam to pickled spiced tomatoes. Less solid jams, which preserve the whole fruits, such as Russian

blackcurrant *varen'ye*, are traditionally served in a small saucer with tea, or to accompany a breakfast bowl of semolina *kasha*.

DRINKS

Russians drink tea that is either imported from the Far East or grown in Georgia. The tea is brewed in a small pot on top of the samovar, and diluted with water from the urn below. In Poland, under strong Central European and Italian influence, coffee is more popular. As for alcohol, both Poland and Russia claim to be the home of vodka, which has been made in Eastern Europe since at least the 15th century. Distilled, ideally from rye, it is then purified and water added. Small additions of barley, oats, buckwheat or wheat, herbs and tree bark give further flavour. Additions to the finished vodka make for specialities such as pepper vodka, which is used as a remedy for colds. Plain vodka is best for the *zakuski* table, however, served ice cold and downed in a single gulp.

Top, clockwise from back: dill, flat-leaved parsley, sour cream, cream, horseradish and fresh garlic bulbs.

Left, clockwise from top left: buckwheat flour, semolina, whole rolled porridge oats, pot barley, millet and raw buckwheat (centre).

SOUPS AND STARTERS

The classic soups of Eastern Europe have remained unchanged for centuries. Shchi, based on cabbage, is a north Russian speciality, while borshch is made from beetroot and is popular in the south and throughout Poland and the Ukraine. The balance of sweet and sour is typical, with the use of fermented juice or pickled vegetables. Many hors d'oeuvres served in the west originated as Russian starters. Caviare is probably the most famous of these, traditionally served with small glasses of ice-cold vodka.

Pea and Barley Soup

This thick and warming soup, *Grochówka*, makes a substantial starter, or it may be served as a meal in its own right, eaten with hot crusty bread.

INGREDIENTS

Serves 6

225g/8oz/1¼ cups yellow split peas
25g/1oz/¼ cup pearl barley
1.75 litres/3 pints/7½ cups vegetable
   or ham stock
50g/2oz smoked streaky bacon, cubed
25g/1oz/2 tbsp butter
1 onion, finely chopped
2 garlic cloves, crushed
225g/8oz celeriac, cubed
15ml/1 tbsp chopped fresh marjoram
salt and freshly ground black pepper
bread, to serve

1 Rinse the peas and barley in a sieve under cold running water. Put in a bowl, cover with plenty of water and leave to soak overnight.

2 The next day, drain and rinse the peas and barley. Put them in a large pan, pour in the stock and bring to the boil. Turn down the heat and simmer gently for 40 minutes.

3 Dry fry the bacon cubes in a frying pan for 5 minutes, or until well browned and crispy. Remove with a slotted spoon, leaving the fat behind, and set aside.

4 Add the butter to the frying pan, add the onion and garlic and cook gently for 5 minutes. Add the celeriac and cook for a further 5 minutes, or until the onion is just starting to colour.

5 Add the softened vegetables and bacon to the pan of stock, peas and barley. Season lightly with salt and pepper, then cover and simmer for 20 minutes, or until the soup is thick. Stir in the marjoram, add extra black pepper to taste and serve with bread.

Borshch

Beetroot is the main ingredient of *Borshch*, and its flavour and colour dominate this well-known soup. It is a classic of both Russia and Poland.

INGREDIENTS

Serves 4–6
900g/2lb uncooked beetroot, peeled
2 carrots, peeled
2 celery sticks
40g/1½ oz/3 tbsp butter
2 onions, sliced
2 garlic cloves, crushed
4 tomatoes, peeled, seeded and chopped
1 bay leaf
1 large parsley sprig
2 cloves
4 whole peppercorns
1.2 litres/2 pints/5 cups beef or chicken stock
150ml/¼ pint/⅔ cup beetroot *kvas* (see *Cook's Tip*) or the liquid from pickled beetroot
salt and freshly ground black pepper
soured cream, garnished with snipped fresh chives or sprigs of dill, to serve

1 Cut the beetroot, carrots and celery into fairly thick strips. Melt the butter in a large pan and cook the onions over a low heat for 5 minutes, stirring occasionally.

2 Add the beetroot, carrots and celery and cook for a further 5 minutes, stirring occasionally.

3 Add the garlic and chopped tomatoes to the pan and cook, stirring, for 2 more minutes.

4 Place the bay leaf, parsley, cloves and peppercorns in a piece of muslin and tie with string.

5 Add the muslin bag to the pan with the stock. Bring to the boil, reduce the heat, cover and simmer for 1¼ hours, or until the vegetables are very tender. Discard the bag. Stir in the beetroot *kvas* and season. Bring to the boil. Ladle into bowls and serve with soured cream garnished with chives or dill.

--- COOK'S TIP ---

Beetroot *kvas*, fermented beetroot juice, adds an intense colour and a slight tartness. If unavailable, peel and grate 1 beetroot, add 150ml/¼ pint/⅔ cup stock and 10ml/2 tsp lemon juice. Bring to the boil, cover and leave for 30 minutes. Strain before using.

Fresh Cabbage Shchi

This version of Russia's national dish is made from fresh cabbage rather than sauerkraut.

INGREDIENTS

Serves 4–6
1 small turnip
2 carrots
40g/1½ oz/3 tbsp butter
1 large onion, sliced
2 celery sticks, sliced
1 white cabbage, about 675g/1½ lb
1.2 litres/2 pints/5 cups beef stock
1 sharp eating apple, cored, peeled
   and chopped
2 bay leaves
5ml/1 tsp chopped fresh dill
10ml/2 tsp pickled cucumber juice
   or lemon juice
salt and freshly ground black pepper
fresh herbs, to garnish
soured cream and black bread, to serve

1 Cut the turnip and carrots into matchstick strips. Melt the butter in a large pan and fry the turnip, carrot, onion and celery for 10 minutes.

2 Shred the cabbage, and add to the pan with the stock, apple, bay leaves and dill and bring to the boil. Cover and simmer for 40 minutes or until the vegetables are really tender.

3 Remove the bay leaves, then stir in the pickled cucumber juice or lemon juice and season with plenty of salt and pepper. Serve hot, garnished with fresh herbs and accompanied by soured cream and black bread.

Sorrel and Spinach Soup

This is an excellent Russian summer soup. If sorrel is unavailable, use double the amount of spinach instead and add a dash of lemon juice to the soup just before serving.

INGREDIENTS

Serves 4
25g/1oz/2 tbsp butter
225g/8oz sorrel, washed and
   stalks removed
225g/8oz young spinach, washed and
   stalks removed
25g/1oz fresh horseradish, grated
750ml/1¼ pints/3 cups *kvas* or cider
1 pickled cucumber, finely chopped
30ml/2 tbsp chopped fresh dill
225g/8oz cooked fish, such as pike,
   perch or salmon, skinned and boned
salt and freshly ground black pepper
sprig of dill, to garnish

1 Melt the butter in a large pan. Add the sorrel and spinach leaves and fresh horseradish. Cover and gently cook for 3–4 minutes, or until the leaves are wilted.

COOK'S TIP

Kvas is a Russian beer made by fermenting wheat, rye and buckwheat.

2 Spoon into a food processor and process to a fine purée. Ladle into a tureen or bowl and stir in the *kvas* or cider, cucumber and dill.

3 Chop the fish into bite-size pieces. Add to the soup, then season with plenty of salt and pepper. Chill for at least 3 hours before serving, garnished with a sprig of dill.

Mixed Mushroom Solyanka

The tart flavours of pickled cucumber, capers and lemon add extra bite to this rich soup.

INGREDIENTS

Serves 4

2 onions, chopped
1.2 litres/2 pints/5 cups vegetable
   stock
450g/1lb/6 cups mushrooms, sliced
20ml/4 tsp tomato purée
1 pickled cucumber, chopped
1 bay leaf
15ml/1 tbsp capers in brine, drained
pinch of salt
6 peppercorns, crushed
lemon rind curls, green olives and
   sprigs of flat leaf parsley, to garnish

1 Put the onions in a large pan with 50ml/2fl oz/¼ cup of the stock. Cook, stirring occasionally, until the liquid has evaporated.

2 Add the remaining vegetable stock with the sliced mushrooms, bring to the boil, cover and simmer gently for 30 minutes.

3 In a small bowl, blend the tomato purée with 30ml/2 tbsp of stock.

4 Add the tomato purée to the pan with the pickled cucumber, bay leaf, capers, salt and peppercorns. Cook gently for 10 more minutes.

5 Ladle the soup into warmed bowls and sprinkle lemon rind curls, a few olives and a sprig of flat leaf parley over each bowl before serving.

Grandfather's Soup

This soup derives its name from the fact that it is easily digested and therefore thought to be suitable for the elderly.

INGREDIENTS

Serves 4

1 large onion, finely sliced
25g/1oz/2 tbsp butter
350g/12oz potatoes, peeled and diced
900ml/1½ pints/3¾ cups beef stock
1 bay leaf
salt and freshly ground black pepper

For the drop noodles

75g/3oz/⅔ cup self-raising flour
pinch of salt
15g/½oz/1 tbsp butter
15ml/1 tbsp chopped fresh parsley,
   plus a little extra to garnish
1 egg, beaten
chunks of bread, to serve

1 In a wide heavy-based pan, cook the onion in the butter gently for 10 minutes, or until it begins to brown.

2 Add the diced potatoes and cook for 2–3 minutes, then pour in the stock. Add the bay leaf, salt and pepper. Bring to the boil, then reduce the heat, cover and simmer for 10 minutes.

COOK'S TIP

Use old potatoes, of a floury texture, such as King Edward or Maris Piper.

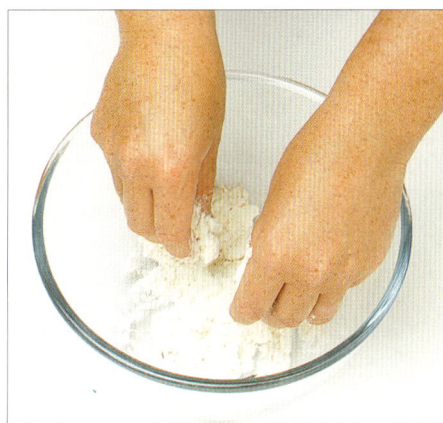

---

3 Meanwhile, make the noodles. Sift the flour and salt into a bowl and rub in the butter. Stir in the parsley, then add the egg to the flour mixture and mix to a soft dough.

4 Drop half-teaspoonfuls of the dough into the simmering soup. Cover and simmer gently for a further 10 minutes. Ladle the soup into warmed soup bowls, scatter over a little parsley, and serve immediately with chunks of bread.

Creamy Kohlrabi Soup

Kohlrabi has always been a popular Polish vegetable, since it tolerates frost and can be stored for a long time. *Zupa z Kalarepy* is a good example of how it can form the basis for simple, hearty dishes.

INGREDIENTS

Serves 4

450g/1lb kohlrabi
25g/1oz/2 tbsp butter
1 onion, roughly chopped
600ml/1 pint/2½ cups
   vegetable stock
600ml/1 pint/2½ cups milk
1 bay leaf
25g/1oz/¼ cup small pasta shapes
salt and freshly ground black pepper

1 Peel and dice the kohlrabi and set aside.

COOK'S TIP

Kohlrabi are usually sold trimmed; if you find them with leaves, shred them if large and use as a garnish, either raw or steamed.

2 Melt the butter in a large pan. Add the onion and cook gently for 10 minutes, or until soft. Add the diced kohlrabi and cook for 2 minutes.

3 Add the vegetable stock, milk and bay leaf to the pan. Bring to the boil, then cover and simmer for 25 minutes, or until the kohlrabi is tender. Let cool for a few minutes and remove the bay leaf.

4 Purée the soup until smooth (you may need to do this in batches) and season with salt and pepper. Bring to the boil, then sprinkle in the pasta. Cover and simmer for 10 minutes, or until the pasta is cooked. Serve with bread.

Creamed Mushrooms

This Russian starter, traditionally made with ceps, is delicious served with warm plain *blini*.

INGREDIENTS

Serves 4

450g/1lb/6 cups mushrooms
50g/2oz/4 tbsp butter
1 small onion, finely sliced
300ml/½ pint/1¼ cups soured cream
30ml/2 tbsp chopped fresh dill
salt and freshly ground black pepper
warm, plain blini, to serve

1 Rinse the mushrooms under cold water. Drain well, then slice thinly.

2 Melt the butter in a frying pan and cook the sliced onion for 5 minutes.

3 Add the sliced mushrooms to the pan and cook over a high heat for 3 minutes, stirring all the time.

4 Stir in the soured cream and chopped dill. Season with plenty of salt and pepper. Bring to the boil and simmer for 1 minute. Serve immediately, with warm blini.

Eggs with Caviare

Caviare is the roe from the huge sturgeon fish that swim in the Caspian Sea. It is often served on its own, in a bowl set over crushed ice, with a glass of chilled neat vodka. Alternatively, it may be used sparingly, as in this Ukrainian recipe, as a garnish.

INGREDIENTS

Serves 4
6 eggs, hard-boiled and halved, lengthways
4 spring onions, very finely sliced
30ml/2 tbsp mayonnaise
1.5ml/¼ tsp Dijon mustard
25g/1oz/2 tbsp caviare or black lumpfish roe
salt and freshly ground black pepper
small sprigs of dill, to garnish
watercress, to serve

1 Remove the yolks from the halved eggs. Mash the yolks to a smooth paste in a bowl with the spring onions, mayonnaise and mustard. Mix well and season with salt and pepper.

2 Fill the egg whites with the yolk mixture and arrange them on a serving dish. Spoon a little caviare or roe on top of each before serving with watercress.

TYPES OF CAVIARE

Beluga is the largest member of the sturgeon family, and the eggs are a pearly-grey colour. **Oscietra** comes from a smaller sturgeon, and the eggs have a golden tinge. **Sevruga** caviare is less expensive than other types, as it produces eggs at a much younger age. **Lumpfish roe,** not a true caviare, has black or orange eggs. **Salmon roe**, from the red salmon, has large, translucent pinky-orange eggs.

Aubergine "Caviare"

The word "caviare" is used to describe spreads and dips made from cooked vegetables. The aubergine is the vegetable most widely used in this way, and many Ukrainian families have their own secret recipe.

INGREDIENTS

Serves 4–6
1.5kg/3lb aubergines
1 onion, very finely chopped
1 garlic clove, crushed
75ml/5 tbsp olive oil
450g/1lb tomatoes, peeled and chopped
5ml/1 tsp lemon juice
150ml/¼ pint/⅔ cup natural yogurt
5ml/1 tsp salt
freshly ground black pepper
spring onion slices, to garnish
toasted bread twists, to serve

1 Preheat the oven to 180°C/350°F/ Gas 4. Put the aubergines on an oiled rack over a roasting tin. Bake in the oven for 25–30 minutes, or until soft. Leave to cool.

2 Meanwhile, fry the finely chopped onion and garlic in 15ml/1 tbsp of the oil for 10 minutes.

3 Using a spoon, remove the baked aubergine flesh, then purée in a food processor until smooth. With the motor running, add the remaining oil.

4 Spoon into a bowl. Stir in the onions, tomatoes, lemon juice and yogurt, salt and pepper to taste. Cover with clear film and chill for 4 hours. To serve, garnish with spring onions and accompany with toasted bread twists.

Herring Pâté

Vast quantities of herring are fished in the Baltic Sea to the north of Poland. A traditional Polish hors d'oeuvre, *Pasta Śledziowa* is usually served with tiny glasses of ice-cold vodka.

INGREDIENTS

Serves 4
2 fresh herrings, filleted
50g/2oz/4 tbsp butter, softened
5ml/1 tsp creamed horseradish sauce
freshly ground black pepper

To serve
4 slices rye bread
1 small onion, cut into rings
1 red eating apple, cored and sliced
15ml/1 tbsp lemon juice
45ml/3 tbsp soured cream

1 Chop the herrings into pieces and put in a food processor with the butter, horseradish sauce and pepper. Process until smooth.

2 Spoon the herring pâté into a bowl. Cover with clear film and chill for at least 1 hour.

3 Serve the pâté on rye bread, add onion rings and apple slices, tossed in lemon juice. Top with a little soured cream and garnish with dill.

Little Finger Biscuits

These savoury Polish biscuits, *paluszki*, are delicious served warm or cold with soup or dips, or on their own as a snack.

INGREDIENTS

Makes 30
115g/4oz/8 tbsp butter, softened
115g/4oz/1⅓ cups mashed potato
150g/5oz/1¼ cups plain flour, plus extra for dusting
2.5ml/½ tsp salt
1 egg, beaten
30ml/2 tbsp caraway seeds

1 Preheat the oven to 220°C/425°F/ Gas 7. Put the butter and mashed potato in a large bowl. Sift the flour and salt into the bowl, then mix to a soft dough.

2 Knead the dough on a lightly floured surface for a few seconds, or until smooth. Wrap in clear film and chill for 30 minutes.

3 Roll out the potato dough on a lightly floured surface until 8mm/⅓in thick. Brush with beaten egg, then cut into strips 2 × 7.5cm/ ¾ × 3in. Transfer to an oiled baking sheet and sprinkle with caraway seeds.

4 Bake for 12 minutes, or until lightly browned. Transfer to a wire rack and leave to cool. Store in an airtight container.

Pirozhki

Homemade *pirozhki* are great favourites of old and young alike. They look splendid piled high and golden brown.

INGREDIENTS

Makes 35
225g/8oz/2 cups strong white flour
2.5ml/½ tsp salt
2.5ml/½ tsp caster sugar
5ml/1 tsp easy-blend dried yeast
25g/1oz/2 tbsp butter, softened
1 egg, beaten, plus a little extra
90ml/6 tbsp warm milk

For the filling

1 small onion, finely chopped
175g/6oz minced chicken
15ml/1 tbsp sunflower oil
75ml/5 tbsp chicken stock
30ml/2 tbsp chopped fresh parsley
pinch of grated nutmeg
salt and freshly ground black pepper

1 Sift the flour, salt and sugar into a large bowl. Stir in the dried yeast, then make a well in the centre.

2 Add the butter, egg and milk and mix to a soft dough. Turn on to a lightly floured surface and knead for 10 minutes, until smooth and elastic.

3 Put the dough in a clean bowl, cover with clear film and leave in a warm place to rise for 1 hour, or until the dough has doubled in size.

4 Meanwhile, fry the onion and chicken in the oil for 10 minutes. Add the stock and simmer for 5 minutes. Stir in the parsley, nutmeg and salt and pepper. Leave to cool.

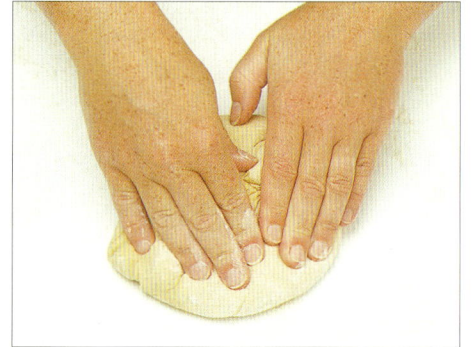

5 Preheat the oven to 220°C/425°F/ Gas 7. Knead the dough, then roll out until 3mm/⅛in thick. Stamp out rounds with a 7.5cm/3in cutter.

6 Brush the edges with beaten egg. Put a little filling in the middle, then press the edges together. Leave to rise on oiled baking sheets, covered with oiled clear film, for 15 minutes. Brush with a little more egg. Bake for 5 minutes, then for 10 minutes at 190°C/375°F/ Gas 5, until well risen.

Buckwheat Blini

Traditionally eaten during the meatless week before Lent, both sweet and savoury toppings can be used; soured cream and caviare is the most famous.

INGREDIENTS

Serves 4
75g/3oz/²/₃ cup plain flour
50g/2oz/½ cup buckwheat or
  wheatmeal flour
2.5ml/½ tsp salt
5ml/1 tsp easy-blend dried yeast
175ml/6fl oz/³/₄ cup warm milk
25g/1oz/2 tbsp butter, melted
1 egg, separated
45ml/3 tbsp oil

For the toppings
150ml/5fl oz/²/₃ cup soured cream
30ml/2 tbsp chopped fresh dill
50g/2oz/4 tbsp red or black
  lumpfish roe
115g/4oz smoked mackerel, skinned,
  boned and flaked
50g/2oz/4 tbsp unsalted butter,
  softened
finely grated rind of ½ lemon
shredded lemon rind, to garnish
lemon wedges, to serve

1 Sift the flours and salt into a large bowl, adding any bran left in the sieve. Stir in the easy-blend yeast, then make a well in the centre.

2 Pour in the milk and gradually beat in the flour until smooth. Cover with clear film and leave to rise for 1 hour, or until doubled in size.

3 Stir in the melted butter and egg yolk. Whisk the egg white in a bowl until stiff and then gently fold in. Cover and leave to stand for 20 minutes.

4 Heat 15ml/1 tbsp of the oil in a large, heavy frying pan over a medium heat and drop in about 4 spoonfuls of batter. Cook for 1–2 minutes, or until bubbles appear on top.

5 Turn them over and cook for a further 1 minute, or until both sides are brown. Remove the *blini* from the pan and keep them moist in a folded clean dish towel.

6 Repeat the process with the remaining batter, adding a little oil to the pan when needed, to make about 24 *blini*. Allow to cool.

7 Arrange the *blini* on a serving plate. Use the soured cream and chopped dill to top half of the *blini*. Spoon 5ml/ 1 tsp lumpfish roe on top of the soured cream and dill.

8 In another bowl, mix the smoked mackerel, butter and lemon rind together and use to top the remaining *blini*. Garnish with shredded lemon rind. Serve with lemon wedges.

Olivier Salad

In the 1880s the French chef, Olivier, opened a restaurant in Moscow called the Hermitage. It became one of the most famous dining clubs in the city, where many innovative dishes were served. Olivier later published a book of everyday Russian cooking and gave his name to this elaborate salad.

INGREDIENTS

Serves 6
2 young grouse or partridges
6 juniper berries, crushed
40g/1½oz/3 tbsp butter, softened
2 small onions, each stuck with
    3 cloves
2 streaky bacon rashers, halved
10 baby potatoes, unpeeled
1 cucumber
2 Little Gem lettuces, separated
    into leaves
2 eggs, hard-boiled and quartered

For the dressing
1 egg yolk
5ml/1 tsp Dijon mustard
175ml/6fl oz/¾ cup light olive oil
60ml/4 tbsp white wine vinegar
salt and freshly ground black pepper

1 Preheat the oven to 200°C/400°F/ Gas 6. Put the grouse or partridges in a small roasting tin. Mix the juniper berries and the butter together and tuck half the juniper butter and one clove-studded onion into the vent of each of the birds.

2 Lay 2 bacon pieces over each breast. Roast for 30 minutes, or until the juices run only slightly pink when the thigh is pierced with a skewer.

3 Leave to cool, then cut the meat into 2.5cm/1in pieces.

4 Meanwhile, cook the potatoes in boiling salted water for about 20 minutes, or until tender. Allow to cool, then peel and cut into 1cm/½in slices.

COOK'S TIP

Cold roast beef can be used instead of the game, if you prefer.

---

5 Cut a few slices of cucumber for garnishing and set aside. Halve the remaining cucumber lengthways, remove the seeds and dice.

6 To make the dressing, put the egg yolk, mustard and a little salt and pepper in a small bowl and whisk together. Add the olive oil in a thin stream, whisking all the time until thickened, then stir in the vinegar.

7 Put the pieces of meat, potato and cucumber in a bowl. Pour over half the dressing and mix carefully. Arrange the lettuce leaves on a serving platter and pile the salad in the middle.

8 Garnish with the reserved cucumber slices and the quartered hard-boiled eggs. Serve with the remaining dressing.

MEAT AND POULTRY

Although beef, poultry and game are eaten in Russia, Poland and the Ukraine, pork is by far the most popular meat. Whole joints are usually marinated to produce tender and succulent meat, and pork is the main ingredient of kielbasa, the famous Polish sausage exported all over the world. Throughout the region, frequent food shortages in history have called for ingenuity in making a little go a long way, and many recipes reflect this by cleverly combining a number of meats with herbs, spices and pickled vegetables.

Liver and Bacon Varenyky

There is an old Ukrainian superstition that if *varenyky* are counted, the dough will split and the filling spill out.

INGREDIENTS

Serves 4
200g/7oz/1¾ cups plain flour
1.5ml/¼ tsp salt
2 eggs, beaten
15g/½ oz/1 tbsp butter, melted
beaten egg, for sealing
15ml/1 tbsp sunflower oil

For the filling
15ml/1 tbsp sunflower oil
½ small onion, finely chopped
115g/4oz smoked streaky bacon, roughly chopped
225g/8oz chicken or lamb's liver, roughly chopped
30ml/2 tbsp snipped fresh chives, plus extra for garnish
salt and freshly ground black pepper

1 Sift the flour and salt into a bowl. Make a well in the centre. Add the eggs and butter and mix to a dough.

2 Knead the dough on a lightly floured surface for 2–3 minutes, until smooth. Wrap in clear film and leave to rest for 30 minutes.

3 For the filling, heat the oil in a pan and cook the onion for 5 minutes. Add the bacon and cook for a further 4–5 minutes. Stir in the liver and cook for 1 minute, until browned.

4 Put the liver mixture in a food processor or blender and process until it is finely chopped, but not smooth. Add the snipped chives and season with salt and pepper. Process for a few more seconds.

5 Roll out the dough on a lightly floured surface until 3mm/⅛ in thick. Stamp out rounds of dough with a 5cm/2in cutter.

6 Spoon a teaspoon of filling into the middle of each round. Brush the edges of the dough with beaten egg and fold in half to make half-moon shapes. Leave to dry on a floured dish towel for 30 minutes.

7 Bring a pan of salted water to the boil. Add the oil, then add the *varenyky*, in batches if necessary. Bring back to the boil and cook them at a gentle simmer for 10 minutes, until tender. Drain well and serve hot, garnished with snipped chives. Serve with fresh capers.

Roast Loin of Pork with Apple Stuffing

A spit-roasted sucking pig, basted with butter or cream and served with an apple in its mouth, was a classic dish for the Russian festive table. This roasted loin with crisp crackling makes a less expensive alternative.

INGREDIENTS

Serves 6–8
1.75kg/4lb boned loin of pork
300ml/$\frac{1}{2}$ pint/$1\frac{1}{4}$ cups dry cider
150ml/$\frac{1}{4}$ pint/$\frac{2}{3}$ cup soured cream
7.5ml/$1\frac{1}{2}$ tsp sea salt

For the stuffing
25g/1oz/2 tbsp butter
1 small onion, chopped
50g/2oz/1 cup fresh white
  breadcrumbs
2 apples, cored, peeled and chopped
50g/2oz/scant $\frac{1}{2}$ cup raisins
finely grated rind of 1 orange
pinch of ground cloves
salt and freshly ground black pepper

1 Preheat the oven to 220°C/425°F/ Gas 7. To make the stuffing, melt the butter in a pan and gently fry the onion for 10 minutes, or until soft. Stir into the remaining stuffing ingredients.

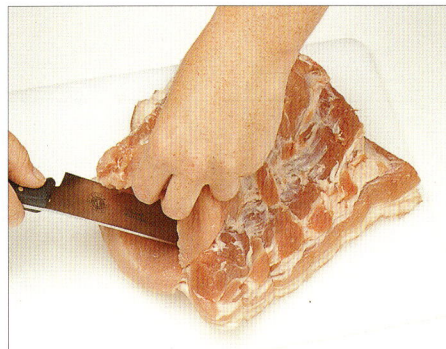

2 Put the pork, rind side down, on a board. Make a horizontal cut between the meat and outer layer of fat, cutting to within 2.5cm/1in of the edges to make a pocket.

3 Push the stuffing into the pocket. Roll up lengthways and tie with string. Score the rind at 2cm/$\frac{3}{4}$in intervals with a sharp knife.

— COOK'S TIP —

Do not baste during the final 2 hours of roasting, so that the crackling becomes crisp.

4 Pour the cider and soured cream into a casserole, in which the joint just fits. Stir to combine, then add the pork, rind side down. Cook, uncovered, in the oven for 30 minutes.

5 Turn the joint over, so that the rind is on top. Baste with the juices, then sprinkle the rind with sea salt. Cook for 1 hour, basting after 30 minutes.

6 Reduce the oven temperature to 180°C/350°F/Gas 4. Cook for a further $1\frac{1}{2}$ hours. Leave the joint to stand for 20 minutes before carving.

Russian Hamburgers

Every Russian family has its own version of this homely hamburger. The mixture can also be shaped into small round meatballs known as *bitki*, which make irresistible snacks.

INGREDIENTS

Serves 4
115g/4oz/2 cups fresh white
  breadcrumbs
45ml/3 tbsp milk
450g/1lb finely minced beef, lamb
  or veal
1 egg, beaten
30ml/2 tbsp plain flour
30ml/2 tbsp sunflower oil
salt and freshly ground black pepper
tomato sauce, pickled vegetables and
  crispy fried onions, to serve

1 Put the breadcrumbs in a bowl and spoon over the milk. Leave to soak for 10 minutes. Add the minced meat, egg, salt and pepper and mix all the ingredients together thoroughly.

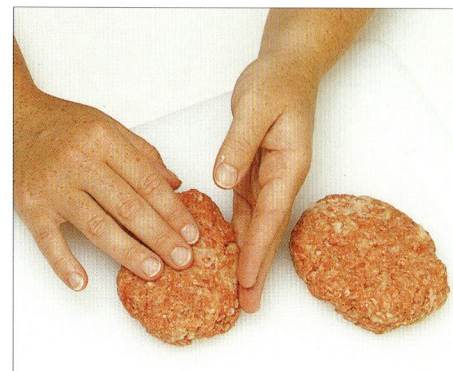

2 Divide the mixture into 4 equal portions and shape into ovals, each about 10cm/4in long and 5cm/2in wide. Coat each with the flour.

3 Heat the oil in a frying pan and fry the burgers for about 8 minutes on each side. Serve with a tomato sauce, pickled vegetables and fried onions.

Beef Stroganov

At the end of the 19th century, Alexander Stroganov gave his name to this now well-known Russian dish of beef and onions cooked with cream, and it became his signature dish when entertaining at his home in Odessa. Finely cut potato chips are the classic accompaniment.

INGREDIENTS

Serves 4
450g/1lb fillet or rump steak, trimmed
15ml/1 tbsp sunflower oil
25g/1oz/2 tbsp unsalted butter
1 onion, sliced
15ml/1 tbsp plain flour
5ml/1 tsp tomato purée
5ml/1 tsp Dijon mustard
5ml/1 tsp lemon juice
150ml/¼ pint/⅔ cup soured cream
salt and freshly ground black pepper
fresh herbs, to garnish

1 Place the steak between 2 oiled sheets of clear film. Gently beat with a rolling pin to flatten and tenderize the meat. Cut it into thin strips about 5cm/2in long.

2 Heat the remaining oil and half the butter in a frying pan and fry the beef over a high heat for 2 minutes, or until browned. Remove the strips of beef from the pan with a slotted spoon, leaving any juices behind.

3 Melt the remaining butter in the pan and gently fry the onion for 10 minutes, until soft.

4 Sprinkle over the flour then stir it in, followed by the tomato purée, mustard, lemon juice and soured cream. Return the beef to the pan and stir until the sauce is bubbling. Season to taste with salt and pepper, and then serve immediately, garnished with fresh herbs, with deep-fried potato chips.

Bigos

Poland's national dish, *bigos*, is best made a day in advance.

INGREDIENTS

Serves 8

15g/¹⁄₂oz/¹⁄₄ cup dried mushrooms
225g/8oz/1 cup stoned prunes
225g/8oz lean boneless pork
225g/8oz lean boneless venison
225g/8oz chuck steak
225g/8oz *kielbasa* (see Cook's Tip)
25g/1oz/¹⁄₄ cup plain flour
2 onions, sliced
45ml/3 tbsp olive oil
60ml/4 tbsp dry Madeira
900g/2lb can or packet sauerkraut, rinsed
4 tomatoes, peeled and chopped
4 cloves
5cm/2in cinnamon stick
1 bay leaf
2.5ml/¹⁄₂ tsp dill seeds
600ml/1 pint/2¹⁄₂ cups stock
salt and freshly ground black pepper

1 Pour boiling water to completely cover the dried mushrooms and prunes in a bowl. Leave for 30 minutes, then drain well.

2 Cut the pork, venison, chuck steak and *kielbasa* sausage into 2.5cm/1in cubes, then toss together in the flour. Gently fry the onions in the oil for 10 minutes. Remove.

3 Brown the meat in the pan in several batches, for about 5 minutes, or until well browned; remove and set aside. Add the Madeira and simmer for 2–3 minutes, stirring.

4 Return the meat to the pan with the onion, sauerkraut, tomatoes, cloves, cinnamon, bay leaf, dill seeds, mushrooms and prunes. Pour in the stock and season with salt and pepper.

5 Bring to the boil, cover and simmer gently for 1³⁄₄–2 hours, or until the meat is very tender. Uncover for the last 20 minutes to let the liquid evaporate, as the stew should be thick. Sprinkle with chopped parsley. Serve immediately with boiled new potatoes, tossed in chopped parsley.

COOK'S TIP

Kielbasa is a garlic-flavoured pork and beef sausage, but any similar type of continental sausage can be used. Use porcini mushrooms, if possible.

Kovbasa

These Ukrainian pork and beef sausages can be made several days ahead and kept refrigerated.

INGREDIENTS

Serves 6
450g/1lb pork, such as shoulder
225g/8oz chuck steak
115g/4oz pork back fat
2 eggs, beaten
30ml/2 tbsp *peperivka* (see *Cook's Tip*)
  or pepper vodka
2.5ml/½ tsp ground allspice
5ml/1 tsp salt
about 1.75 litres/3 pints/7½ cups
  chicken stock
fresh parsley, to garnish
mashed potato, to serve

1 Mince the meats and pork back fat together, using the coarse blade of a mincer, then mince half the mixture again, this time using a fine blade.

2 Combine both the meat mixtures with the eggs, *peperivka*, allspice and salt. Check the seasoning by frying a small piece of the mixture, then tasting it. Adjust if necessary.

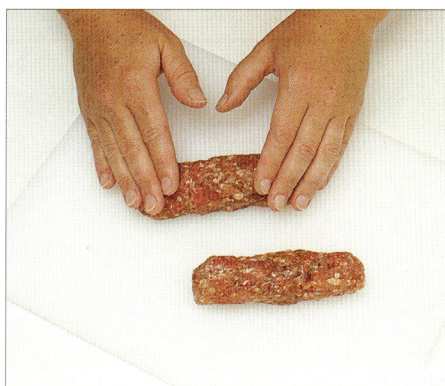

COOK'S TIP

Spicing whisky with peppers to make *peperivka* is an old tradition in the Ukraine. Add 3 whole cayenne peppers, pricked all over with a fine skewer, to 150ml/¼ pint/ ⅔ cup whisky or bourbon and leave for at least 48 hours.

---

3 Form the meat mixture into 2 sausages, about 20cm/8in long. Wrap in double muslin and tie securely with string.

4 Bring the stock to a gentle simmer in a large pan. Add the sausages and simmer gently, turning frequently, for 35–40 minutes, or until the juices run clear when the sausages are pierced with a fine skewer.

5 Leave the sausages in the stock for 20 minutes, then remove and leave to cool. Remove the muslin and sauté the sausages in oil to brown them. Garnish with parsley and serve with mashed potato, topped with butter.

Field-roasted Lamb

This unusual recipe, originally for mutton slowly roasted over charcoal, comes from the Russian steppes.

INGREDIENTS

Serves 6

1.75kg/4lb leg of lamb
4 large garlic cloves, cut into slivers
5ml/1 tsp whole peppercorns
300ml/½ pint/1¼ cups natural yogurt
15ml/1 tbsp olive oil
15ml/1 tbsp chopped fresh dill
300ml/½ pint/1¼ cups lamb or
　　vegetable stock
30ml/2 tbsp lemon juice
potatoes, spinach and carrots, to serve

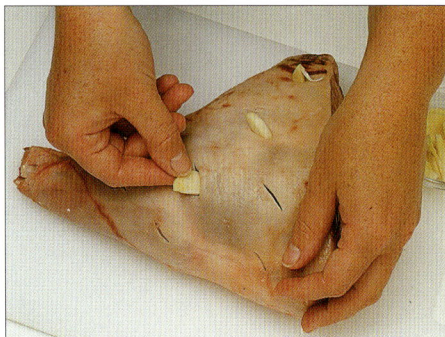

1 Make slits all over the lamb and insert generous slivers of fresh garlic into the slits.

2 Lightly crush the whole peppercorns in a pestle and mortar or rolling pin, if preferred.

3 Tip the yogurt, oil and crushed peppercorns into a bowl, then add the dill and mix together well.

4 Spread the yogurt paste evenly over the lamb. Put the lamb in a glass dish, cover loosely with foil and then refrigerate the lamb for 1–2 days, turning it twice.

5 Transfer the lamb to a roasting tin and let it come back to room temperature. Preheat the oven to 220°C/425°F/Gas 7. Remove the foil. Pour in the stock and lemon juice and cook, uncovered, for 20 minutes.

6 Reduce the oven temperature to 180°C/350°F/Gas 4 and continue roasting for a further 1¼–1½ hours, basting occasionally. Remove from the oven and keep covered in a warm place for 15–20 minutes before carving. Use the juices from the pan to make a gravy and serve with roast potatoes, boiled spinach and baby carrots.

Lamb Plov

Plov is the Russian name for this rice dish popular throughout Eastern Europe, known by different names – *pilau* in Turkey and *pilaf* in the Middle East.

INGREDIENTS

Serves 4

50g/2oz/scant ½ cup raisins
115g/4oz/½ cup stoned prunes
15ml/1 tbsp lemon juice
25g/1oz/2 tbsp butter
1 large onion, chopped
450g/1lb lamb fillet, trimmed and cut into 1cm/½in cubes
225g/8oz lean minced lamb
2 garlic cloves, crushed
600ml/1 pint/2½ cups lamb or vegetable stock
350g/12oz/scant 2 cups long-grain rice
large pinch of saffron
salt and freshly ground black pepper
sprigs of flat leaf parsley, to garnish

1 Put the raisins and prunes in a small bowl and pour over enough water to cover. Add the lemon juice and leave to soak for at least 1 hour. Drain, then roughly chop the prunes.

2 Meanwhile, heat the butter in a large pan and cook the onion for 5 minutes. Add the lamb fillet, minced lamb and garlic. Fry for 5 minutes, stirring constantly until browned.

3 Pour in 150ml/¼ pint/⅔ cup of the stock. Bring to the boil, then lower the heat, cover and simmer for 1 hour, or until the lamb is tender.

4 Add the remaining stock and bring to the boil. Add the rice and saffron. Stir, then cover and simmer for 15 minutes, or until the rice is tender.

5 Stir in the raisins, chopped prunes, salt and pepper. Heat through for a few minutes, then turn on to a warmed serving dish and garnish with sprigs of flat leaf parsley.

Golubtsy

These tasty Polish cabbage parcels are packed with a herby meat and grain stuffing. They are equally good made with minced lamb, beef or pork.

INGREDIENTS

Serves 4

1 large Savoy cabbage
30ml/2 tbsp sunflower oil
450g/1lb lean minced lamb, beef or pork
1 onion, finely chopped
5ml/1 tsp ground coriander
75ml/5 tbsp stock
115g/4oz/²⁄₃ cup cooked long-grain rice or buckwheat
30ml/2 tbsp chopped fresh parsley
25g/1oz/2 tbsp butter, melted
300ml/½ pint/1¼ cups soured cream
30ml/2 tbsp tomato purée
1 bay leaf
salt and freshly ground black pepper

1 Preheat the oven to 180°C/350°F/ Gas 4. Carefully remove 12 outer leaves from the cabbage one at a time. Blanch them in a pan of boiling salted water for 4 minutes. Drain and pat dry on kitchen paper, then trim away the thick stalks.

2 To make the stuffing, heat half the oil in a frying pan. Add the meat and brown, stirring, for 5 minutes. Remove and set aside. Add the remaining oil and cook the onion for 5 minutes.

3 Stir in the coriander, then add the meat, stock, rice or buckwheat, half the parsley, salt and pepper. Simmer for 5 minutes.

4 Place 30ml/2 tbsp of stuffing on each leaf and wrap it up, tucking in the sides to make a parcel. Arrange in one layer in a greased ovenproof dish. Brush with melted butter.

5 Heat the soured cream, tomato purée and bay leaf gently, stirring until bubbling. Stir in the remaining parsley and season with salt and pepper.

6 Pour the sauce around the stuffed cabbage parcels and cover the dish with foil. Bake for 35 minutes, uncovering for the last 15 minutes, to allow the cabbage to brown.

COOK'S TIP

Instead of blanching the cabbage leaves in water, they can be softened by stacking them on top of each other, wrapping them in oiled foil, then baking at 180°C/350°F/ Gas 4 for 6 minutes.

Meatballs in Mushroom Sauce

These finely minced herby Russian meatballs, flavoured with vodka, are gently poached in a tasty stock.

INGREDIENTS

Serves 4
50g/2oz/4 tbsp butter
1 onion, roughly chopped
30ml/2 tbsp plain flour
150ml/¼ pint/⅔ cup milk
450g/1lb lean minced beef
30ml/2 tbsp vodka
1 egg
2.5ml/½ tsp salt
30ml/2 tbsp chopped fresh coriander
30ml/2 tbsp chopped fresh parsley
900ml/1½ pints/3¾ cups stock
2 bay leaves
freshly ground black pepper
sprigs of coriander, to garnish
plain boiled rice, to serve

For the sauce
25g/1oz/2 tbsp butter
115g/4oz/1½ cups small button
  mushrooms, halved
150ml/¼ pint/⅔ cup soured cream
salt and freshly ground black pepper

1 Melt the butter in a small pan and gently fry the onion for 5 minutes. Stir in the flour and cook for 2 minutes, stirring all the time. Remove the pan from the heat.

2 Gradually add the milk. Return the pan to the heat, bring to the boil and simmer for 2–3 minutes, until thick. Allow to cool for 10 minutes.

3 Tip the sauce into a food processor or blender. Add the minced beef, vodka, egg, salt and a little pepper and process until fairly smooth. Add the herbs and process for a few more seconds, until well mixed.

4 Bring the stock and bay leaves to the boil. Drop in 10 heaped teaspoonfuls of the meat mixture. Remove when they rise to the surface, then add the next batch. You will make about 30 meatballs.

5 To make the sauce, melt the butter in a large pan and fry the mushrooms for 5 minutes. Stir in the soured cream and bring to the boil. Season to taste. Add the meatballs to the sauce and warm through. Garnish with coriander and serve with boiled rice.

— COOK'S TIP —

The meatballs can be shallow fried in 2.5cm/1in sunflower oil, if preferred.

Chicken Bitki

Chicken is one of the most popular meats eaten in Poland. Use guinea fowl to mimic the gamey flavour of Polish chicken.

INGREDIENTS

Makes 12
15g/½oz/1 tbsp butter, melted
115g/4oz flat mushrooms, finely chopped
50g/2oz/1 cup fresh white breadcrumbs
350g/12oz chicken breasts or guinea fowl, minced or finely chopped
2 eggs, separated
1.5ml/¼ tsp grated nutmeg
30ml/2 tbsp plain flour
45ml/3 tbsp oil
salt and freshly ground black pepper
green salad and grated pickled beetroot, to serve

1 Melt the butter in a pan and fry the mushrooms for 5 minutes until soft and all the juices have evaporated. Allow to cool.

2 Mix the crumbs, chicken, yolks, nutmeg, salt and pepper and flat mushrooms well.

3 Whisk the egg whites until stiff. Stir half into the chicken mixture, then fold in the remainder.

4 Shape the mixture into 12 even meatballs, about 7.5cm/3in long and 2.5cm/1in wide. Roll in the flour to coat.

5 Heat the oil in a frying pan and fry the *bitki* for 10 minutes, turning until evenly golden brown and cooked through. Serve hot with a green salad and pickled beetroot.

Chicken Kiev

This popular recipe is a modern Russian invention. These deep fried chicken breasts filled with garlic butter should be prepared well in advance to allow time for chilling.

INGREDIENTS

Serves 4
115g/4oz/8 tbsp butter, softened
2 garlic cloves, crushed
finely grated rind of 1 lemon
30ml/2 tbsp chopped fresh tarragon
pinch of freshly grated nutmeg
4 chicken breast fillets with wing bones attached, skinned
1 egg, lightly beaten
115g/4oz/2 cups fresh breadcrumbs
oil, for deep frying
salt and freshly ground black pepper
lemon wedges, to garnish
potato wedges, to serve

1 Mix the butter in a bowl with the garlic, lemon rind, tarragon and nutmeg. Season to taste with salt and pepper. Shape the butter into a rectangular block about 5cm/2in long, wrap in foil and chill for 1 hour.

2 Place the chicken, skinned sides down, on a piece of oiled clear film. Cover with a second piece of clear film and gently beat the pieces with a rolling pin until fairly thin.

3 Cut the butter lengthways into four pieces and put one in the centre of each chicken fillet. Fold the edges over the butter and secure with wooden cocktail sticks.

4 Tip the beaten egg and the breadcrumbs into separate small dishes. Dip the chicken pieces first in the beaten egg and then in the breadcrumbs to coat evenly. Dip them a second time in egg and crumbs, then put on a plate and refrigerate for at least 1 hour.

5 Heat the oil in a large pan or deep fat fryer to 180°C/350°F. Deep fry the chicken for 6–8 minutes, or until the chicken is cooked and the coating golden brown and crisp. Drain on kitchen paper and remove the cocktail sticks. Serve hot, garnished with wedges of lemon and potato wedges.

Chicken and Pork Terrine

Serve this delicate Ukrainian pâté with warm, crusty bread.

INGREDIENTS

Serves 6–8
225g/8oz rindless, streaky bacon
375g/13oz boneless chicken
  breast, skinned
15ml/1 tbsp lemon juice
225g/8oz lean minced pork
½ small onion, finely chopped
2 eggs, beaten
30ml/2 tbsp chopped fresh parsley
5ml/1 tsp salt
5ml/1 tsp green peppercorns, crushed
fresh green salad, radishes and lemon
  wedges, to serve

1 Preheat the oven to 160°C/325°F/ Gas 3. Put the bacon on a board and stretch it using the back of a knife so that it can be arranged in over-lapping slices over the base and sides of a 900g/2lb loaf tin.

2 Cut 115g/4oz of the chicken into strips about 10cm/4in long. Sprinkle with lemon juice. Put the rest of the chicken in a food processor or blender with the minced pork and the onion. Process until fairly smooth.

3 Add the eggs, parsley, salt and peppercorns to the meat mixture and process again briefly. Spoon half the mixture into the loaf tin and then level the surface.

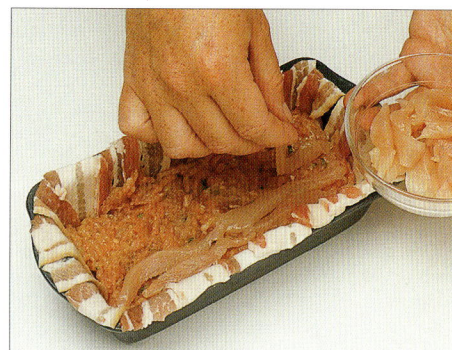

4 Arrange the chicken strips on top, then spoon in the remaining meat mixture and smooth the top. Give the tin a couple of sharp taps to knock out any pockets of air.

5 Cover with a piece of oiled foil and put in a roasting tin. Pour in enough hot water to come halfway up the sides of the loaf tin. Bake for about 45–50 minutes, until firm.

6 Allow the terrine to cool in the tin before turning out and chilling. Serve sliced, with a fresh green salad, baby tomatoes and wedges of lemon to squeeze over.

Roast Duckling with Honey

A sweet and sour orange sauce is the perfect foil for this rich-tasting Polish duck recipe, and frying the orange rind intensifies the flavour.

INGREDIENTS

Serves 4

2.25kg/5lb oven-ready duckling
2.5ml/½ tsp ground allspice
1 orange
15ml/1 tbsp sunflower oil
30ml/2 tbsp plain flour
150ml/¼ pint/⅔ cup chicken or
  duck stock
10ml/2 tsp red wine vinegar
15ml/1 tbsp clear honey
salt and freshly ground black pepper
watercress and thinly pared orange
  rind, to serve

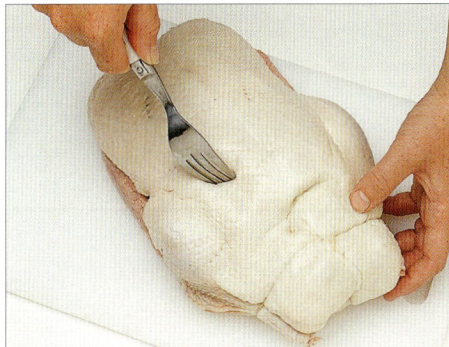

1 Preheat the oven to 220°C/425°F/ Gas 7. Using a fork, pierce the duckling all over, except the breast, so that the fat runs out during cooking

2 Rub all over the skin of the duckling with allspice and sprinkle with salt and pepper.

3 Put the duckling on a rack over a roasting tin and cook for about 20 minutes. Next reduce the oven temperature to 190°C/375°F/Gas 5 and cook for a further 2 hours.

4 Meanwhile, thinly pare the rind from the orange and cut into very fine strips. Heat the oil in a pan and gently fry the orange rind for 2–3 minutes. Squeeze the juice from the orange and set aside.

5 Transfer the duckling to a warmed serving dish and keep warm. Drain off all but 30ml/2 tbsp fat from the tin, sprinkle in the flour and stir well.

6 Stir in the stock, vinegar, honey, orange juice and rind. Bring to the boil, stirring all the time. Simmer for 2–3 minutes. Season the sauce and serve the duckling with watercress and thinly pared orange rind.

FISH

The seas to the north and south and the vast lakes and the rivers that flow across this region provide an abundance of fish, which are cooked in wonderful ways. Russia's most famous export, caviare, comes from the huge sturgeon that swim in the Caspian Sea. The Baltic provides this region with herring, which is served in many guises throughout the year since it is well suited to pickling. However, freshwater fish predominate, including eel, perch, tench and salmon, but the favourites are pike and carp, which are always served on feast days.

Pike and Salmon Mousse

When sliced, this light-textured Russian mousse loaf, *Pate iz Shchuki*, reveals a pretty layer of pink salmon. For a special occasion, serve topped with red salmon caviare.

INGREDIENTS

Serves 8

225g/8oz salmon fillets, skinned
600ml/1 pint/2½ cups fish stock
finely grated rind and juice of
 ½ lemon
900g/2lb pike fillets, skinned
4 egg whites
475ml/16fl oz/2 cups double cream
30ml/2 tbsp chopped fresh dill
salt and freshly ground black pepper
red salmon caviare or dill sprig,
 to garnish (optional)

1 Preheat the oven to 180°C/350°F/ Gas 4. Line a 900g/2lb loaf tin with greaseproof paper and brush with oil.

2 Cut the salmon into 5cm/2in strips. Place the stock and lemon juice in a pan and bring to the boil, then turn off the heat. Add the salmon strips, cover and leave for 2 minutes. Remove with a slotted spoon.

3 Cut the pike into cubes and process in a food processor or blender until smooth. Lightly whisk the egg whites with a fork. With the motor running, slowly pour in the egg whites, then the cream. Finally, add the lemon rind, dill and seasoning.

4 Spoon half of the pike mixture into the prepared loaf tin.

5 Arrange the poached salmon strips on top, then carefully spoon in the remaining pike mixture.

6 Cover the loaf tin with foil and put in a roasting tin. Add enough boiling water to come halfway up the sides of the loaf tin. Bake for 45–50 minutes, or until firm.

7 Leave on a wire rack to cool, then chill for at least 3 hours. Turn out on to a serving plate and remove the lining paper. Serve the mousse cut in slices and garnished with red salmon caviare or a sprig of dill, if liked.

Salmon Kulebyaka

A Russian festive dish in which a layer of moist salmon and eggs sits on a bed of buttery dill-flavoured rice, all encased in crisp puff pastry.

INGREDIENTS

Serves 4
50g/2oz/4 tbsp butter
1 small onion, finely chopped
175g/6oz/1 cup cooked long-
   grain rice
15ml/1 tbsp chopped fresh dill
15ml/1 tbsp lemon juice
450g/1lb puff pastry, defrosted
   if frozen
450g/1lb salmon fillet, skinned and cut
   into 5cm/2in pieces
3 eggs, hard-boiled and chopped
beaten egg, for sealing and glazing
salt and freshly ground black pepper
watercress, to garnish

1 Preheat the oven to 200°C/400°F/ Gas 6. Melt the butter in a pan, add the finely chopped onion and cook gently for 10 minutes, or until soft.

2 Stir in the cooked rice, dill, lemon juice, salt and pepper.

3 Roll out the puff pastry on a lightly floured surface to a 30cm/12in square. Spoon the rice mixture over half the pastry, leaving a 1cm/½in border around the edges.

4 Arrange the salmon on top, then scatter the eggs in between.

5 Brush the pastry edges with egg, fold it over the filling to make a rectangle, pressing the edges together firmly to seal.

6 Carefully lift the pastry on to a lightly oiled baking sheet. Glaze with beaten egg, then pierce the pastry a few times with a skewer to make holes for the steam to escape.

7 Bake on the middle shelf of the oven for 40 minutes, covering with foil after 30 minutes. Leave to cool on the baking sheet, before cutting into slices. Garnish with watercress.

Braised Tench and Vegetables

Freshwater tench is the smallest member of the carp family, with a sweet firm flesh and few bones. In this simple Polish recipe, the combination of vegetables can easily be adapted to suit an individual's taste or seasonal availability.

INGREDIENTS

Serves 4
900g/2lb tench, filleted
    and skinned
15ml/1 tbsp lemon juice
75g/3oz/6 tbsp butter
1 onion, halved and cut into wedges
1 celery stick, sliced
1 carrot, halved lengthways and sliced
115g/4oz/1½ cups small button
    mushrooms, halved
50ml/2fl oz/¼ cup vegetable stock
salt and freshly ground black pepper

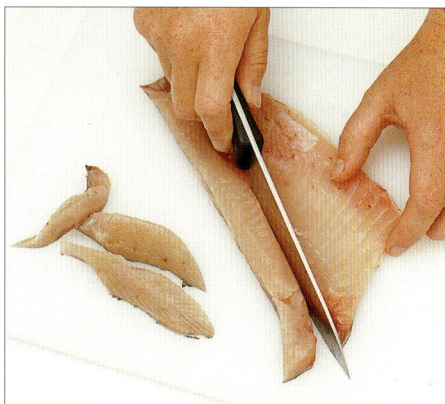

1 Cut the fish fillets into strips about 2.5cm/1in wide. Sprinkle them with the lemon juice and a little salt and pepper and set aside.

2 Melt the butter in a large flameproof casserole and cook the onion wedges for 5 minutes. Add the celery, carrot and mushrooms and cook for a further 2–3 minutes, stirring to coat in the butter.

3 Pour the stock into the pan. Place the fish on top of the vegetables in a single layer. Cover the casserole with a lid and cook over a very low heat for 25–30 minutes, until the fish and vegetables are tender.

VARIATION

Use small carp in this recipe if liked. Carp has a slightly earthier flavour.

Plaice in Polish Sauce

This sauce is Polish only in name, not in origin. A mixture of recipes, it is a quick and simple sauce to prepare, that goes well with any poached, grilled or steamed fish.

INGREDIENTS

Serves 4
4 plaice fillets, about 225g/8oz each
75g/3oz/6 tbsp butter
2 eggs, hard-boiled and
    finely chopped
30ml/2 tbsp chopped fresh dill
15ml/1 tbsp lemon juice
salt and freshly ground black pepper
lemon slices, to garnish
boiled baby carrots, to serve

1 Put the fish, skin side down, on a sheet of greased foil on a grill rack. Melt the butter in a small pan and brush a little over the fish. Season with salt and pepper.

2 Grill the fish under a moderate heat for 8–10 minutes, or until just cooked. Transfer to a warmed plate.

3 Add the eggs, dill and lemon juice to the melted butter in the pan. Heat gently for 1 minute. Pour over the fish just before serving. Garnish with lemon slices and serve with boiled baby carrots.

Fish Babka

This fish pudding is lightened with egg whites, giving it a soufflé-like texture. It is much more stable, however, and can be turned out to serve.

INGREDIENTS

Serves 4

350g/12oz white fish fillets, skinned and cut into 2.5cm/1in cubes
50g/2oz white bread, cut into 1cm/½in cubes
250ml/8fl oz/1 cup milk
25g/1oz/2 tbsp butter
1 small onion, finely chopped
3 eggs, separated
1.5ml/¼ tsp grated nutmeg
salt and freshly ground black pepper
30ml/2 tbsp chopped fresh dill, plus extra to garnish
sliced courgettes and carrots, to serve

1 Preheat the oven to 180°C/350°F/ Gas 4. Base-line with greaseproof paper and butter a 1.5 litre/2½ pint/ 6¼ cup ovenproof dish.

2 Place the fish cubes in a bowl. Add the bread, then sprinkle over the milk and leave to soak while you cook the chopped onion.

3 Melt the butter in a small pan and fry the onion for 10 minutes, until soft. Cool for a few minutes, then add to the fish and bread with the egg yolks, nutmeg, dill, salt and pepper. Mix well.

4 Whisk the egg whites in a large bowl until stiff, then gently fold into the fish mixture.

5 Spoon the mixture into the dish. Cover with buttered foil and bake for 45 minutes, or until set.

6 Allow to stand for 5 minutes, then spoon out. Alternatively, loosen with a knife; turn out, remove the paper and cut into wedges. Garnish with dill and serve with courgettes and carrots.

Muscovite Solyanka

This layered fish and vegetable bake has the same name as one of Russia's classic soups. The name reflects the prevalent "sourness" of the ingredients.

INGREDIENTS

Serves 4

675g/1½ lb eel, skinned and boned
900ml/1½ pints/3¾ cups fish or
    vegetable stock
1.2 litres/2 pints/5 cups water
450g/1lb/4 cups shredded
    white cabbage
50g/2oz/4 tbsp butter
1 large onion, chopped
2 pickled cucumbers, sliced
12 green olives
15ml/1 tbsp capers, drained
75g/3oz/1½ cups fresh white
    breadcrumbs
salt and freshly ground black pepper

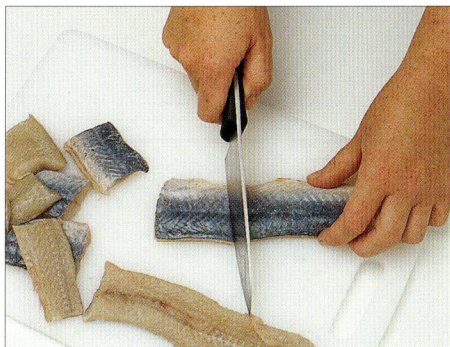

1 Cut the eel into large pieces. Bring the stock to a gentle simmer in a large pan, add the eel and cook for 4 minutes. Remove with a slotted spoon. Reserve 150ml/¼ pint/⅔ cup of the stock and set aside, leaving the remaining stock in the pan.

2 Pour the water into the pan of stock. Bring to the boil, then add the cabbage. Simmer for 2 minutes, then strain well.

3 Melt half of the butter in the pan. Fry the onion for 5 minutes.

4 Stir in the strained cabbage and reserved stock, then bring to the boil. Cover with a tight-fitting lid and cook over a low heat for 1 hour, until tender. Season with salt and pepper.

5 Preheat the oven to 200°C/400°F/ Gas 6. Spoon half the cabbage into a baking dish. Top with the eel and the cucumbers. Spoon over the remaining cabbage and any remaining stock.

6 Scatter the olives, capers and the breadcrumbs over the top. Melt the remaining butter and drizzle over the top. Bake for 25–30 minutes, or until lightly browned. Garnish with parsley sprigs and serve with boiled potatoes.

Rolled Fish Fillets

Whiting or sea perch can also be used in this dish. Their delicate flavour is complemented by the lemon and thyme.

INGREDIENTS

Serves 4

8 sole fillets, about 200g/7oz, skinned
45ml/3 tbsp olive oil
15ml/1 tbsp lemon juice
25g/1oz/2 tbsp butter
175g/6oz/2 cups button mushrooms, very finely chopped
4 anchovy fillets, finely chopped
5ml/1 tsp chopped fresh thyme, plus extra to garnish
2 eggs, beaten
115g/4oz/2 cups white breadcrumbs
oil, for deep frying
salt and freshly ground black pepper
grilled chicory, to serve

1 Lay the fish fillets in a single layer in a glass dish. Mix together the oil and lemon juice and sprinkle over. Cover with clear film and marinate in the refrigerator for at least 1 hour.

2 Melt the butter in a pan and gently fry the mushrooms for 5 minutes, until tender and all the juices have evaporated. Stir in the chopped anchovies, thyme, salt and pepper.

3 Divide the mixture equally and spread evenly over the fish. Roll up and secure with cocktail sticks.

— COOK'S TIP —

To skin the fillets, slice the flesh away from the skin using a sharp knife. Keep the knife parallel to the fish and the skin taut.

4 Dip each fish roll in beaten egg, then in breadcrumbs to coat. Repeat this process. Heat the oil to 180°C/350°F/Gas 4.

5 Deep fry in 2 batches for 4–5 minutes, or until well browned and cooked through. Drain on kitchen paper. Remove the cocktail sticks and sprinkle with thyme. Serve with grilled chicory.

Carp with Green Horseradish Sauce

Carp is a freshwater fish much used in Polish cooking, and it is traditional Christmas fare.

INGREDIENTS

Serves 4

675g/1½lb carp, skinned and filleted
45ml/3 tbsp plain flour
1 egg, beaten
115g/4oz/2 cups fresh white breadcrumbs
sunflower oil, for frying
salt and freshly ground black pepper
lemon wedges, to serve

For the sauce

15g/½oz fresh horseradish, finely grated
pinch of salt
150ml/¼ pint/⅔ cup double cream
1 bunch of watercress, trimmed and finely chopped
30ml/2 tbsp snipped fresh chives
2 eggs, hard-boiled and finely chopped (optional)

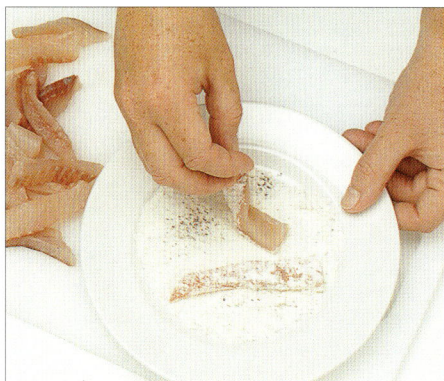

1 Cut the fish into thin strips, about 6cm/2½in long by 1cm/½in thick. Season the flour with salt and pepper. Dip the strips of fish in the flour, then in the beaten egg and finally in the breadcrumbs.

2 Heat 1cm/½in of oil in a frying pan. Fry the fish in batches for 3–4 minutes, until golden brown. Drain on kitchen paper and keep warm until all the strips are cooked.

3 For the sauce, put the horseradish, salt, cream and watercress in a small pan. Bring to the boil and simmer for 2 minutes. Stir in the chives and eggs, if using Serve the sauce with the fish

Baked Cod with Horseradish Sauce

Baking fish in a sauce keeps it moist. In this Ukrainian recipe, a second, tangy sauce is served alongside for added flavour.

INGREDIENTS

Serves 4
4 thick cod fillets or steaks
15ml/1 tbsp lemon juice
25g/1oz/2 tbsp butter
25g/1oz/¼ cup plain flour, sifted
150ml/¼ pint/⅔ cup milk
150ml/¼ pint/⅔ cup fish stock
salt and freshly ground black pepper
parsley sprigs, to garnish
potato wedges and chopped spring
  onions, fried, to serve

For the horseradish sauce
30ml/2 tbsp tomato purée
30ml/2 tbsp grated fresh horseradish
150ml/¼ pint/⅔ cup soured cream

1 Preheat the oven to 180°C/350°F/ Gas 4. Place the fish in a buttered ovenproof dish in a single layer. Sprinkle with lemon juice.

2 Melt the butter in a small heavy-based pan. Stir in the flour and cook for 3–4 minutes until lightly golden. Stir to stop the flour sticking to the pan. Remove from the heat.

3 Gradually whisk the milk, and then the stock, into the flour mixture. Season with salt and pepper. Bring to the boil, stirring, and simmer for 3 minutes, still stirring.

4 Pour the sauce over the fish and bake for 20–25 minutes, depending on the thickness. Check by inserting a skewer in the thickest part: the flesh should be opaque.

5 For the horseradish sauce, blend the tomato purée and horseradish with the soured cream in a small pan. Slowly bring to the boil, stirring, and then simmer for 1 minute.

6 Pour the horseradish sauce into a serving bowl and serve alongside the fish. Serve the fish hot. Garnish with the parsley sprigs and serve with the potato wedges and fried chopped spring onions.

Glazed Pike-perch

This Russian fish dish, with its glistening aspic coating, makes an impressive centrepiece for a formal occasion.

INGREDIENTS

Serves 8–10

2.25–2.75kg/5–6lb whole pike-perch
30ml/2 tbsp sunflower oil
2 bay leaves
8 whole peppercorns
1 lemon, sliced
300ml/$\frac{1}{2}$ pint/1$\frac{1}{4}$ cups white wine
25g/1oz sachet aspic jelly
2 cucumbers, halved and thinly sliced
salt and freshly ground black pepper
dill sprigs and lemon wedges,
    to garnish
mayonnaise, to serve

1 Wash the pike-perch under cold running water. Snip off the fins with sharp scissors. Season the inside of the fish with salt and pepper. Brush the skin with the oil to protect it from the heat during cooking.

2 Put the fish on the trivet of a fish kettle or on a rack in a large roasting tin. Add the bay leaves, peppercorns and lemon slices. Pour over the wine and enough water to cover.

3 Cover with a lid or a piece of oiled foil. Bring to the boil and simmer very gently for 10 minutes. Turn off the heat and leave the pike-perch to cool with the lid still on. When cool peel the skin off the fish, leaving the head and tail intact.

4 Prepare the aspic with boiling water, according to the packet instructions. Cool and brush generously over the fish.

5 Arrange the cucumber slices over the fish, then brush again with aspic. Allow to set before serving, garnished with dill sprigs and lemon wedges.

--- COOK'S TIP ---

A whole fresh salmon or salmon trout can be cooked in exactly the same way.

VEGETABLES, GRAINS AND PASTA

Served on their own or as an accompaniment, vegetables in Russia, Poland and the Ukraine reflect the cold climate. Cabbage, beetroot, swede and turnip are the staples, often preserved by salting or pickling. Mushrooms are popular, too, since huge forests cover much of the region and gathering them is a favourite pastime. Potatoes also feature, particularly in Polish cooking, although grains, especially buckwheat, rye and barley, are more widely eaten. Surprisingly, stuffed pasta is traditional, usually with meat or cheese fillings.

Potato Cakes

Although not as widely used as cereals, potatoes feature often in Polish recipes. They were introduced during the reign of Jan Sobieski, in the 17th century.

INGREDIENTS

Serves 4

450g/1lb potatoes, peeled and cut into
    large chunks
25g/1oz/2 tbsp butter
1 small onion, chopped
45ml/3 tbsp soured cream
2 egg yolks
25g/1oz/¼ cup plain flour
1 egg, beaten
25g/1oz/½ cup fresh white
    breadcrumbs
salt and freshly ground black pepper

1 Preheat the oven to 180°C/350°F/ Gas 4. Cook the potatoes in a pan of boiling salted water for 20 minutes, or until tender. Drain well and mash. Allow to cool for a few minutes. Meanwhile, melt the butter in a small pan and fry the onion for 10 minutes, until soft.

2 Stir the butter and onion into the mashed potato and then mix in the cream and egg yolks.

3 Sift the flour over the potato mixture, then mix it in well. Season with plenty of salt and pepper. Shape into rounds, then flatten slightly to make about 16 "doughnuts" 6cm/ 2½in across.

4 Place the "doughnuts" on a lightly oiled baking sheet and brush with beaten egg. Sprinkle the tops with breadcrumbs. Bake for 30 minutes, or until browned.

Pampushki

When these crunchy Russian potato dumplings are split open, a tasty curd cheese and chive filling is revealed.

INGREDIENTS

Serves 4
675g/1½ lb potatoes, peeled
225g/8oz/2⅔ cups cooked
  mashed potato
2.5ml/½ tsp salt
75g/3oz/scant ½ cup curd cheese
30ml/2 tbsp snipped fresh chives
freshly ground black pepper
oil, for deep frying

1 Coarsely grate the raw potatoes and squeeze out as much water as possible. Put them in a bowl with the mashed potato, salt and black pepper. Mix together. In another bowl, mix the curd cheese and chives together.

2 Using a spoon and your fingers, scoop up a portion of the potato mixture, slightly smaller than an egg, and then flatten to a circle.

3 Put 5ml/1 tsp of the cheese filling into the middle, then fold over the edges and pinch to seal. Repeat with remaining potato and cheese mixtures, to make about 12 dumplings.

4 Heat the oil to 170°C/340°F. Deep fry the dumplings for 10 minutes, or until deep brown and crisp. Drain on kitchen paper and serve hot.

COOK'S TIP

Pampushki are traditionally cooked in stock or water and served with soup. If you prefer to poach them, add 15ml/1 tbsp plain flour and 1 beaten egg to the mixture and poach the dumplings for 20 minutes.

Galushki

One of the most popular Ukrainian dishes, *galushki* are pieces of a pasta-like dough, cooked in milk or stock. Healthy and filling, they can be made from wheat flour, buckwheat flour, semolina or potatoes.

INGREDIENTS

Serves 4
225g/8oz/2 cups plain flour
1.5ml/¼ tsp salt
25g/1oz/2 tbsp butter, melted
2 eggs, beaten
1 vegetable stock cube
115g/4oz lardons or smoked streaky
  bacon, rinded and chopped,
  to serve

1 Sift the flour and salt into a bowl. Make a well in the centre. Add the butter and eggs and mix to a dough.

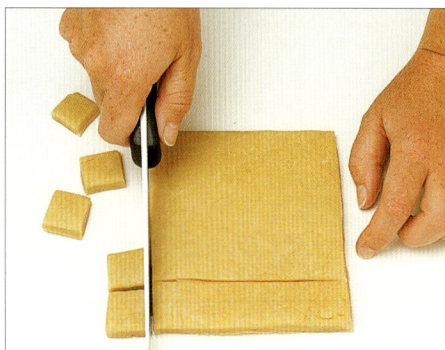

2 Knead on a lightly floured surface until smooth. Wrap in clear film and leave to rest for 30 minutes. Roll out on a lightly floured surface until 1cm/½in thick, and cut into 2cm/¾in squares using a sharp knife or a pastry wheel. Leave to dry on a floured dish towel for 30 minutes.

3 Crumble the stock cube into a pan of gently boiling water. Add the *galushki* and simmer for 10 minutes, or until cooked. Drain well.

4 Meanwhile, dry fry the lardons or bacon in a non-stick frying pan for 5 minutes, until brown and crispy. Serve scattered over the *galushki*.

Cheese Dumplings

Easily prepared, dumplings are common additions to soups throughout the Ukraine. They are also served with meats and on their own as a simple supper.

INGREDIENTS

Serves 4
115g/4oz/1 cup self-raising flour
25g/1oz/2 tbsp butter
25g/1oz/⅓ cup crumbled feta, dry
  brinza (sheep's milk cheese), or a
  mixture of Caerphilly and Parmesan
30ml/2 tbsp chopped fresh herbs
60ml/4 tbsp cold water
salt and freshly ground black pepper
parsley sprigs, to garnish

For the topping
40g/1½oz/3 tbsp butter
50g/2oz/1 cup slightly dry white
  breadcrumbs

1 Sift the flour into a bowl. Rub in the butter until the mixture resembles fine breadcrumbs.

2 Stir the cheese and herbs into the mixture. Season with salt and pepper. Add the cold water and mix to a firm dough; then shape into 12 balls.

3 Bring a pan of salted water to the boil. Add the dumplings, cover and gently simmer for 20 minutes, until light and fluffy.

4 For the topping, melt the butter in a frying pan. Add the breadcrumbs and cook for 2–3 minutes, until the crumbs are golden and crisp. Remove the dumplings with a slotted spoon and sprinkle with breadcrumbs. Serve garnished with parsley sprigs.

Drachena

A Russian cross between an omelette and a pancake, this is a savoury *drachena,* but it is often served as a dessert by leaving out the vegetables and sweetening with sugar or honey.

INGREDIENTS

Serves 2–3
15ml/1 tbsp olive oil
1 bunch spring onions, sliced
1 garlic clove, crushed
4 tomatoes, peeled, seeded
  and chopped
45ml/3 tbsp wholemeal rye flour
60ml/4 tbsp milk
150ml/¼ pint/⅔ cup soured cream
4 eggs, beaten
30ml/2 tbsp chopped fresh parsley
25g/1oz/2 tbsp butter, melted
salt and freshly ground black pepper
green salad, to serve

1 Preheat the oven to 180°C/350°F/ Gas 4. Heat the oil in a frying pan and gently cook the spring onions for 3 minutes. Add the garlic and cook for 1 more minute, or until the spring onions are soft.

2 Sprinkle the spring onions and garlic into the base of a lightly greased shallow 20cm/8in ovenproof dish and scatter over the tomatoes.

3 Mix the flour to a smooth paste in a bowl with the milk. Gradually add the soured cream, then mix with the eggs. Stir in the parsley and melted butter. Season with salt and pepper.

4 Pour the egg mixture over the vegetables. Bake in the oven for 40–45 minutes, or until hardly any liquid seeps out when a knife is pushed into the middle.

5 Run a knife around the edge of the dish to loosen, then cut into wedges and serve immediately with a fresh green salad.

Braised Barley and Vegetables

One of the oldest of cultivated cereals, pot barley has a nutty flavour and slightly chewy texture. It makes a warming and filling dish when combined with root vegetables.

INGREDIENTS

Serves 4
225g/8oz/1 cup pearl or pot barley
30ml/2 tbsp sunflower oil
1 large onion, chopped
2 celery sticks, sliced
2 carrots, halved lengthways and sliced
225g/8oz swede or turnip, cut into
   2cm/³/₄ in cubes
225g/8oz potatoes, cut into 2cm/
   ³/₄ in cubes
475ml/16fl oz/2 cups vegetable stock
salt and freshly ground black pepper
celery leaves, to garnish

1 Put the barley in a measuring jug and add water to reach the 600ml/ 1 pint/2¹/₂ cup mark. Leave to soak in a cool place for at least 4 hours or, preferably, overnight.

2 Heat the oil in a large pan and fry the onion for 5 minutes. Add the sliced celery and carrots and cook for 3–4 minutes, or until the onion is starting to brown.

3 Add the barley and its soaking liquid to the pan. Then add the swede or turnip, potato and stock to the barley. Season with salt and pepper. Bring to the boil, then reduce the heat and cover the pan.

4 Simmer for 40 minutes, or until most of the stock has been absorbed and the barley is tender. Stir occasionally towards the end of cooking to prevent the barley from sticking to the base of the pan. Serve, garnished with celery leaves.

Buckwheat Kasha

Kasha is a type of Russian porridge, made from a variety of grains including wheat, barley, millet and oats. The most popular is buckwheat, which has a distinctive nutty flavour.

INGREDIENTS

Serves 4
175g/6oz/scant 1 cup buckwheat
750ml/1¼ pints/3 cups boiling stock
25g/1oz/2 tbsp butter
pinch of freshly grated nutmeg
115g/4oz smoked streaky bacon,
  rinded and chopped
salt and freshly ground black pepper

1 Dry fry the buckwheat in a non-stick frying pan for 2 minutes, or until very lightly toasted. Add the stock.

— COOK'S TIP —

Buckwheat *kasha* is equally good with the addition of fried mushrooms and makes an excellent stuffing for roast chicken. Buckwheat is often sold already roasted, in which case there is no need to dry fry it before adding the stock.

2 Simmer very gently for 15–20 minutes, stirring occasionally to prevent it sticking. When almost dry, remove from the heat.

3 Add the butter to the buckwheat and season with nutmeg, salt and pepper. Cover the pan with a lid and leave to stand for 5 minutes.

4 Meanwhile, dry fry the bacon in a non-stick pan for 5 minutes, until lightly browned and crispy. Sprinkle over the kasha before serving.

Carters' Millet

This dish was originally cooked over an open fire by carters who travelled across the steppes of southern Ukraine.

INGREDIENTS

Serves 4
225g/8oz/scant 1¼ cups millet
600ml/1 pint/2½ cups
  vegetable stock
115g/4oz lardons or smoked streaky
  bacon, rinded and chopped
15ml/1 tbsp olive oil
1 small onion, thinly sliced
225g/8oz/3 cups small field
  mushrooms, sliced
15ml/1 tbsp chopped fresh mint
salt and freshly ground black pepper

1 Rinse the millet in a sieve under cold running water. Put in a pan with the stock, bring to the boil and simmer, covered, for 30 minutes, until the stock has been absorbed.

2 Dry fry the bacon in a non-stick pan for 5 minutes, or until brown and crisp. Remove and set aside.

3 Add the oil to the pan and cook the onion and mushrooms for 10 minutes, until beginning to brown.

4 Add the bacon, onion and mushrooms to the millet. Stir in the mint and season with salt and pepper. Heat gently for 1–2 minutes before serving.

Beetroot Casserole

This Russian vegetarian casserole can be served as a light meal in itself. Its sweet and sour flavour also makes it an ideal dish to serve with roasted chicken or game.

INGREDIENTS

Serves 4

50g/2oz/4 tbsp butter
1 onion, chopped
2 garlic cloves, crushed
675g/1½lb uncooked beetroot, peeled
2 large carrots, peeled
½ lemon
115g/4oz/1½ cups button mushrooms
300ml/½ pint/1¼ cups
   vegetable stock
2 bay leaves
15ml/1 tbsp chopped fresh mint, plus
   sprigs to garnish (optional)
salt and freshly ground black pepper

For the hot dressing

150ml/¼ pint/⅔ cup soured cream
2.5ml/½ tsp paprika, plus extra
   to garnish

1 Melt the butter in a non-aluminium pan and gently fry the onion and garlic for 5 minutes. Meanwhile, dice the beetroot and carrot. Finely grate the rind and squeeze the juice of the ½ lemon. Add the beetroot, carrots and mushrooms and fry for 5 minutes.

COOK'S TIP

Wear clean rubber or plastic gloves to avoid staining your hands when preparing beetroot. Cooking beetroot in aluminium pans may cause discoloration of pan and food.

2 Pour in the stock with the lemon rind and bay leaves. Season with salt and pepper. Bring to the boil, turn down the heat, cover and simmer for 1 hour, or until the vegetables are soft.

3 Turn off the heat and stir in the lemon juice and chopped mint, if using. Leave the pan to stand, covered, for 5 minutes, to develop the flavours.

4 Meanwhile, for the dressing, gently heat the soured cream and paprika in a small pan, stirring all the time, until bubbling. Transfer the beetroot mixture to a serving bowl, then spoon over the soured cream. Garnish with sprigs of mint and extra paprika, if liked, and serve.

Uszka

Uszka, meaning "little ears", are plump mushroom dumplings, traditionally served in Poland with clear soups. They are also delicious on their own, tossed in a little melted butter and chopped fresh herbs.

INGREDIENTS

Makes 20
75g/3oz/^{2}/$_{3}$ cup plain flour
pinch of salt
30ml/2 tbsp chopped fresh parsley
1 egg yolk
40ml/2^{1}/$_{2}$ tbsp cold water
fresh parsley, to garnish
clear soup or melted herb butter,
  to serve

For the filling

25g/1oz/2 tbsp butter
^{1}/$_{2}$ small onion, very finely chopped
50g/2oz/1 cup mushrooms,
  finely chopped
1 egg white
15ml/1 tbsp dried white breadcrumbs
salt and freshly ground black pepper

1 Sift the flour and salt into a bowl. Add the chopped parsley, egg yolk and water and mix to a dough. Lightly knead the dough on a floured surface until smooth.

2 To make the filling, melt the butter in a pan. Add the onion and mushrooms and fry over a low heat for 10 minutes, or until the onion is very soft. Leave to cool.

3 Lightly whisk the egg white in a clean bowl with a fork. Add 15ml/ 1 tbsp of the egg white to the mushrooms, together with the dried breadcrumbs, salt and pepper. Mix together well.

4 Roll out the dough very thinly on a floured surface. Cut into 5cm/2in squares using a sharp knife or a pastry wheel, then lightly brush with the remaining egg white.

5 Spoon 2.5ml/^{1}/$_{2}$ tsp of mushroom mixture on to each square. Fold the dough in half to make a triangle, then pinch the outer edges together to seal them.

6 Bring a pan of boiling salted water or stock to a brisk boil. Gently drop in the dumplings a few at a time and simmer for 5 minutes. Drain and add to a clear soup or toss in melted herb butter and serve.

Cucumber Salad

Salting the cucumber draws out some of the moisture, thereby making it firmer. Make sure you rinse it thoroughly before using or the salad will be too salty. This popular Ukrainian dish is an ideal summer accompaniment to a main meal.

INGREDIENTS

Serves 6–8
2 cucumbers, decorated with a
    cannelle knife and thinly sliced
5ml/1 tsp salt
45ml/3 tbsp chopped fresh dill
15ml/1 tbsp white wine vinegar
150ml/¼ pint/⅔ cup soured cream
freshly ground black pepper
1 dill sprig, to garnish

1 Put the cucumber in a sieve or colander set over a bowl and sprinkle with the salt. Leave for 1 hour to drain. Rinse the cucumber well under cold running water, then pat dry with kitchen paper.

2 Put the slices of cucumber in a bowl, add the chopped dill and mix everything together well.

3 In another bowl, stir the vinegar into the soured cream and season the mixture with pepper.

4 Pour the soured cream over the cucumber and chill for 1 hour before turning into a serving dish. Garnish with a sprig of dill and serve.

Grated Beetroot and Celery Salad

Raw beetroot has a lovely crunchy texture. Here in this Russian salad, its flavour is brought out by marinating it in a cider dressing.

INGREDIENTS

Serves 4–6
450g/1lb uncooked beetroot, peeled
    and grated
4 celery sticks, finely chopped
30ml/2 tbsp apple juice
fresh herbs, to garnish

For the dressing
45ml/3 tbsp sunflower oil
15ml/1 tbsp cider vinegar
4 spring onions, finely sliced
30ml/2 tbsp chopped fresh parsley
salt and freshly ground black pepper

1 Toss the beetroot, celery and apple juice together in a bowl to mix.

2 Put all the ingredients for the dressing in a small bowl and whisk with a fork until well blended. Stir half into the beetroot mixture.

3 Drizzle the remaining dressing over the top. Allow the salad to marinate for at least 2 hours before serving, for the fullest flavour. Garnish with fresh herbs.

DESSERTS AND BAKES

Russians, Ukrainians and Poles all have a sweet tooth and this is reflected in the vast number and variety of desserts, cakes, pastries and breads. Special occasions are often marked with particular confections, such as Russian Paskha and Polish Babka. Honey and nuts are plentiful and feature in many sweet dishes. Other popular flavourings are cinnamon, cloves and cardamom, as well as candied fruits, vanilla and lemon peel. Fruit, especially orchard and soft fruit, can be of exceptionally high quality.

Kulich

Kulich is served only at Easter in Russia, often instead of bread. Slice in rounds from the top, with the first slice kept as a lid.

INGREDIENTS

Serves 4

500g/1¼lb/5 cups strong white flour
pinch of salt
5ml/1 tsp ground cinnamon
75g/3oz/scant ½ cup caster sugar
50g/2oz/scant ½ cup raisins
50g/2oz/⅓ cup mixed peel
50g/2oz/⅓ cup almonds, chopped
7g/¼oz sachet easy-blend
   dried yeast
300ml/½ pint/1¼ cups milk
50g/2oz/4 tbsp butter
1 egg, beaten
jam, to serve (optional)

For the icing
115g/4oz/1 cup icing sugar
15ml/1 tbsp lemon juice

1 Sift the flour, salt and cinnamon into a large bowl. Stir in the sugar, raisins, mixed peel, almonds and dried yeast. Make a well in the centre.

2 Gently heat the milk and butter in a pan until melted. Allow to cool until tepid. Reserve 5ml/1 tsp of the beaten egg for glazing, then add the remainder to the dry ingredients with the milk and butter. Mix well to form a soft dough.

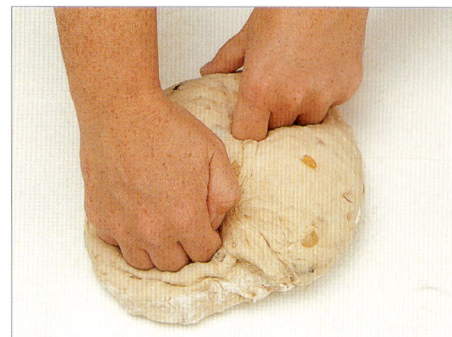

3 Knead the dough on a lightly floured surface for 10 minutes, or until smooth and elastic. Place in a clean bowl, cover with a damp cloth and leave in a warm place to rise for about 1 hour, or until doubled in size.

4 Preheat the oven to 190°C/375°F/ Gas 5. Grease and line a tall cylindrical tin or a deep 20cm/8in round cake tin with greaseproof paper. Turn the dough out and knead again until smooth. Place in the prepared tin, cover with oiled clear film and leave in a warm place until it has risen almost to the top of the tin.

5 Discard the cling film. Brush the top with the reserved egg. Bake for 50–55 minutes, or until a fine skewer inserted into the middle comes out clean. Cover with foil if the *kulich* begins to brown too much. Turn out on to a wire rack to cool.

6 For the icing, sift the icing sugar into a bowl. Add the lemon juice and mix to make a thick icing. Drizzle over the top of the *kulich* and leave to set. Spread with jam, if liked.

Paskha

Paskha is the Russian word for Easter and the name given to this rich curd cheese and candied fruit dessert, which celebrates the end of Lent. Traditionally, it is made in a pyramid-shaped wooden mould with the imprint of the Orthodox cross, but a clean, plastic flowerpot works equally well.

INGREDIENTS

Serves 6–8

115g/4oz/½ cup candied
   fruit, chopped
50g/2oz/scant ½ cup raisins
finely grated rind and juice of 1 lemon
5ml/1 tsp vanilla essence
675g/1½lb/3 cups curd cheese
25g/1oz/2 tbsp unsalted butter
150ml/¼ pint/⅔ cup soured cream
50g/2oz/¼ cup caster sugar
50g/2oz/¼ cup clear honey
50g/2oz/⅓ cup blanched
   almonds, chopped
candied fruits, lemon rind, angelica
   and honey, to decorate

1 Put the candied fruit, raisins, lemon rind and juice and vanilla essence in a small bowl. Stir, then cover and leave to soak for 1 hour.

— COOK'S TIP —

If preferred, drain the mixture for 1 hour in a muslin-lined sieve, before spooning into the lined pudding basin.

2 Meanwhile, line a 1.5 litre/ 2½ pint/6¼ cup plastic flowerpot with a double layer of muslin, allowing the edges to overhang the pot.

3 Put the cheese, butter and soured cream in a mixing bowl and beat until well blended. Add the sugar, honey, blanched almonds and soaked fruits and mix well.

4 Spoon the mixture into the lined flowerpot and fold the edges of the muslin into the middle. Cover with a small plate or saucer that just fits inside the flowerpot, then top with a 450g/ 1lb weight. Stand the flowerpot on a plate and refrigerate overnight.

5 Unfold the muslin, turn the paskha out on to a plate, then remove the muslin. Before serving, decorate with lemon rind, candied fruit and angelica, and drizzle with honey.

Polish Honey Cake

Many Eastern European cakes, like this Polish *Tort Orzechowy*, are sweetened with honey and made with ground nuts and breadcrumbs instead of flour, which gives them a delicious, rich, moist texture.

INGREDIENTS

Serves 12

15g/½oz/1 tbsp unsalted butter, melted and cooled
115g/4oz/2 cups slightly dry fine white breadcrumbs
175g/6oz/¾ cup set honey, plus extra to serve
50g/2oz/¼ cup soft light brown sugar
4 eggs, separated
115g/4oz/1 cup hazelnuts, chopped and toasted, plus extra to decorate

1 Preheat the oven to 180°C/350°F/ Gas 4. Brush a 1.75 litre/3 pint/ 7½ cup fluted brioche tin with the melted butter. Sprinkle with 15g/½oz/ ¼ cup of the breadcrumbs.

--- COOK'S TIP ---

The cake will rise during cooking and sink slightly as it cools – this is quite normal.

2 Put the honey in a large bowl, set over a pan of barely simmering water. When the honey liquifies, add the sugar and egg yolks. Whisk until light and frothy. Remove from the heat.

3 Mix the remaining breadcrumbs with the hazelnuts and fold into the egg yolk and honey mixture. Whisk the egg whites in a separate bowl, until stiff, then gently fold in to the other ingredients, half at a time.

4 Spoon the mixture into the tin. Bake for 40–45 minutes, until golden brown. Leave to cool in the tin for 5 minutes, then turn out on to a wire rack to cool. Scatter over nuts and drizzle with extra honey to serve.

Baked Coffee Custards

Unlike the Russians and Ukrainians, the Polish have a passion for coffee and use it in many of their desserts.

INGREDIENTS

Serves 4
25g/1oz/6 tbsp finely ground coffee
300ml/½ pint/1¼ cups milk
150ml/¼ pint/⅔ cup single cream
2 eggs, beaten
30ml/2 tbsp caster sugar
whipped cream and cocoa powder, to decorate

1 Preheat the oven to 190°C/375°F/ Gas 5. Put the ground coffee in a jug. Heat the milk in a pan until it is nearly boiling. Pour over the coffee and leave to stand for 5 minutes.

2 Strain the coffee-flavoured milk back into the pan. Add the cream and heat again until nearly boiling.

3 Beat the eggs and sugar in a bowl. Pour the hot coffee-flavoured milk into the bowl, whisking all the time. Strain into the rinsed jug.

4 Pour the mixture into 4 × 150ml/ ¼ pint/⅔ cup ramekins. Cover each with a piece of foil.

5 Stand the ramekins in a roasting tin and pour in enough hot water to come halfway up the sides of the ramekins. Bake for 40 minutes, or until lightly set.

6 Remove the ramekins from the roasting tin and allow to cool. Chill for 2 hours. Decorate with a swirl of whipped cream and a sprinkle of cocoa powder, if liked, before serving.

Tort Migdalowy

Almonds are in plentiful supply in Poland and are used in both sweet and savoury dishes. Here they are roasted, giving this coffee-cream-filled sponge a rich and nutty flavour.

INGREDIENTS

Serves 8–10

75g/3oz/½ cup blanched almonds
225g/8oz/1 cup butter, softened
225g/8oz/generous 1 cup caster sugar
4 eggs, beaten
150g/5oz/1¼ cups self-raising flour, sifted

For the icing

175g/6oz/1 cup blanched almonds
40g/1½ oz/9 tbsp ground coffee
75ml/5 tbsp near-boiling water
150g/5oz/¾ cup caster sugar
90ml/6 tbsp water
3 egg yolks
225g/8oz/1 cup unsalted butter

1 Preheat the oven to 190°C/375°F/ Gas 5. Lightly grease and base-line 3 × 18cm/7in round cake tins with greaseproof paper.

2 Put the blanched almonds on a baking sheet and roast in the oven for 7 minutes, or until golden brown.

3 Allow to cool, then transfer to a processor or a blender and process until fine.

4 Cream the butter and sugar together in a bowl until pale and fluffy. Gradually add the eggs, a little at a time, beating well after each addition. Fold in the ground roasted almonds and the flour .

5 Divide the cake mixture evenly between the 3 prepared tins and bake for 25–30 minutes, until well risen and firm to the touch, swapping the position of the top and bottom cakes halfway through cooking. Turn out and cool on a wire rack.

6 For the icing, put the blanched almonds in a bowl and pour over enough boiling water to cover. Leave until cold, then drain the almonds and cut each one lengthways into 4 or 5 slivers with a sharp knife. Roast on a baking sheet for 6–8 minutes.

7 Put the ground coffee in a jug, spoon over the water and leave to stand. Gently heat the sugar and 90ml/ 6 tbsp water in a small heavy-based pan until dissolved. Simmer for 3 minutes, until the temperature reaches 107°C/ 225°F on a sugar thermometer.

8 Put the egg yolks into a bowl and pour over the syrup in a thin stream, whisking all the time until very thick. Cream the butter until soft, then gradually beat the egg mixture into it.

9 Strain the coffee through a sieve and beat into the icing. Use two-thirds to sandwich the cakes together. Spread the remainder over the top and press in the almond slivers.

Raisin Cheesecake

Cheesecakes were originally baked rather than set with gelatine. This Ukrainian dessert is an Easter speciality.

INGREDIENTS

Serves 8
115g/4oz/1 cup plain flour
50g/2oz/4 tbsp butter
15ml/1 tbsp caster sugar
25g/1oz/¼ cup almonds, very
  finely chopped
30ml/2 tbsp cold water
15ml/1 tbsp icing sugar, for dusting

For the filling
115g/4oz/8 tbsp butter
150g/5oz/¾ cup caster sugar
5ml/1 tsp vanilla essence
3 eggs, beaten
25g/1oz/¼ cup plain flour, sifted
400g/14oz/1¾ cups curd cheese
grated rind and juice of 2 lemons
65g/2½oz/½ cup raisins

1 Sift the flour into a bowl. Rub in the butter, until the mixture resembles fine breadcrumbs. Stir in the sugar and almonds. Add the water and mix to a dough. Lightly knead on a floured surface for a few seconds. Wrap in clear film and chill for 30 minutes.

2 Preheat the oven to 200°C/400°F/ Gas 6. Roll out the pastry on a lightly floured surface to a 25cm/10in circle and use it to line the base and sides of a 20cm/8in tart tin. Trim the edges of the pastry with a sharp knife.

3 Prick with a fork, cover with oiled foil and bake for 6 minutes. Remove the foil and bake for 6 more minutes. Allow to cool and reduce the temperature to 150°C/300°F/Gas 2.

4 For the filling, cream the butter, sugar and vanilla essence together. Beat in one egg, then stir in the flour. Beat the cheese until soft, then gradually mix in the remaining eggs. Blend this into the butter mixture. Stir in the lemon rind, juice and raisins.

5 Pour the filling over the pastry base. Bake in the oven for 1½ hours, until firm. Turn off the oven, leave the door ajar and allow to cool before removing. Dust with icing sugar.

Polish Pancakes

Fluffy pancakes are filled with a cheese and sultana mixture.

INGREDIENTS

Makes 6
115g/4oz/1 cup plain flour
pinch of salt
pinch of grated nutmeg, plus extra
   for dusting
1 egg, separated
200ml/7fl oz/scant 1 cup milk
30ml/2 tbsp sunflower oil
25g/1oz/2 tbsp butter
lemon slices, to garnish

For the filling
225g/8oz/1 cup curd cheese
15ml/1 tbsp caster sugar
5ml/1 tsp vanilla essence
50g/2oz/scant ¹/₂ cup sultanas

1 Sift the flour, salt and nutmeg together in a large bowl. Make a well in the centre. Add the yolk and half of the milk. Beat until smooth, then gradually beat in the remaining milk.

2 Whisk the egg white in a bowl until stiff. Fold into the batter.

3 Heat 5ml/1 tsp sunflower oil and a little of the butter in an 18cm/7in frying pan. Pour in enough of the batter to cover the base.

4 Cook for 2 minutes, until golden brown, then turn over and cook for a further 2 minutes.

5 Make 5 more pancakes in the same way, using more oil and butter as necessary. Stack up the pancakes and keep them warm.

6 To make the filling, put the curd cheese, sugar and vanilla essence in a bowl and beat together. Mix in the sultanas. Divide among the pancakes, fold them up and dust with grated nutmeg. Garnish with lemon slices.

Creamy Millet Pudding

The composer Rimsky-Korsakov enjoyed collecting Russian folk-tales. As millet was often featured in them, he famously incorporated the line *A my proso seyali, seyali* ("And we sowed and we sowed millet") into his opera *Snegurochka* (*The Snow Maiden*).

INGREDIENTS

Serves 4

115g/4oz/scant 1 cup millet flakes
600ml/1 pint/2½ cups milk
thinly pared strip of lemon rind
15g/½ oz/1 tbsp butter
30ml/2 tbsp granulated sugar
2 egg whites
plum or apricot jam, to serve

1 Preheat the oven to 180°C/350°F/Gas 4. Put the millet flakes and milk into a small pan. Add the lemon rind and butter, then bring to the boil.

2 Lower the heat and simmer gently for 10 minutes, stirring, until the mixture thickens. Stir in the sugar. Leave to cool for 10 minutes, then remove the lemon rind and discard.

3 Whisk the egg whites in a bowl until stiff. Gently fold into the millet. Spoon into a buttered shallow 1.2 litre/2 pint/5 cup ovenproof dish.

4 Bake for 40–45 minutes, or until the top is golden brown and puffy. Serve hot with plum or apricot jam.

Fruit and Nut Semolina Pudding

This layered dessert was apparently created by Russian Finance Minister, Dmitry Guriev, to honour his country's victory over Napoleon in 1812.

INGREDIENTS

Serves 4

350g/12oz fresh soft fruit, such as
    cherries or plums, stoned and
    chopped
25g/1oz/2 tbsp caster sugar
15ml/1 tbsp water
600ml/1 pint/2½ cups milk
5ml/1 tsp vanilla essence
90ml/6 tbsp semolina
15g/½ oz/1 tbsp soft light
    brown sugar
50g/2oz/½ cup chopped toasted
    hazelnuts or almonds, plus a few
    extra to garnish

1 Put the fruit in a small pan with the caster sugar and water. Cook over a low heat for 8–10 minutes, until the fruit is just soft.

2 Put the milk and vanilla essence in another pan and bring to the boil. Gradually sprinkle in the semolina, whisking all the time. Simmer for 7–8 minutes, or until thick and creamy.

3 Remove from the heat and stir in the soft light brown sugar and chopped nuts. Spoon half the semolina into four individual serving dishes, then top with half the stewed fruit.

4 Spoon over a second layer of semolina. Top with the remaining fruit and the extra nuts. Serve warm or cold.

Paczki

These doughnuts are traditionally eaten in Poland on Shrove Tuesday, at midnight on New Year's Eve, and also at Epiphany (6 January) when a coin is hidden in one of them.

INGREDIENTS

Makes 16
450g/1lb/4 cups plain flour
7g/¼ oz sachet easy-blend
 dried yeast
25g/1oz/2 tbsp butter
75g/3oz/scant ½ cup caster sugar
2 eggs, beaten
150ml/¼ pint/⅔ cup warm water
30ml/2 tbsp dark rum
90ml/6 tbsp plum jam, warmed
 and sieved
oil, for deep frying

For the coating
75g/3oz/scant ½ cup caster sugar
10ml/2 tsp ground cinnamon

1 Sift the flour into a large bowl and stir in the dried yeast. Rub in the butter until the mixture resembles fine breadcrumbs, then stir in the sugar.

2 Make a well in the centre of the mixture, then add the eggs, water and rum, and mix to a soft dough. Turn out on to a lightly floured surface and knead for 10 minutes, or until smooth and elastic.

3 Put the dough in a clean bowl, cover with oiled clear film and leave in a warm place to rise for 1 hour, or until doubled in size.

4 Knead the dough again for 1–2 minutes. Divide into 16 equal pieces and shape each into a ball.

5 Flatten each ball, put 5ml/1 tsp jam in the middle, then gather the edges together over the jam and pinch firmly to seal.

6 Place the dough balls well apart on greased baking sheets and cover with oiled clear film. Leave in a warm place to rise for 30 minutes.

7 Heat the oil in a large pan or deep-fat fryer to 170°C/340°F and fry the doughnuts, a few at a time, for 5 minutes, or until golden brown, turning once during cooking. Drain on kitchen paper.

8 Mix the caster sugar and cinnamon in a bowl. Add the doughnuts one at a time and toss in the mixture to coat. Serve warm.

COOK'S TIP

Allow the doughnuts to cool for at least 10 minutes before serving, as the jam inside will be boiling hot.

Apricot Treat

Fresh fruit was once scarce in Poland during winter, so dried fruits were often used. This rich apricot and almond dessert, a favourite in Poland, resembles the sweetmeats more common to the Balkan regions.

INGREDIENTS

Serves 6
225g/8oz/1 cup ready-to-eat
    dried apricots, chopped
45ml/3 tbsp water
50g/2oz/¼ cup caster sugar
50g/2oz/½ cup chopped almonds
50g/2oz/⅓ cup chopped candied
    orange peel
icing sugar, for dusting
whipped cream, to serve
ground cinnamon, to decorate

1 Put the apricots and water in a heavy-based pan. Cover and simmer, stirring, for about 20 minutes, until a thick paste forms.

2 Stir in the caster sugar and simmer, stirring, for a further 10 minutes until quite dry. Remove from the heat and stir in the almonds and chopped orange peel.

3 Using a knife, shape into a "sausage", about 5cm/2in thick, on a piece of greaseproof paper dusted with icing sugar.

4 Leave to dry in a cool place for at least 3 hours. Cut into slices and serve with whipped cream, sprinkled with a little cinnamon.

Dried Fruit Compote

Fruit grows in abundance in orchards throughout the Ukraine and dried fruits are used all year round. *Uzvar* is served on Christmas Eve and also at feasts at which the dead are honoured. This easy and delicious dessert is also made in Russia.

INGREDIENTS

Serves 6
350g/12oz/2 cups mixed dried fruits,
    such as apples, pears, prunes, peaches
    or apricots
1 cinnamon stick
300ml/½ pint/1¼ cups cider or water
65g/2½oz/½ cup raisins
30ml/2 tbsp clear honey
juice of ½ lemon
mint leaves, to decorate

1 Put the mixed dried fruit in a large pan with the cinnamon and cider or water. Heat gently until almost boiling, then cover the pan, lower the heat and cook gently for 12–15 minutes, to soften the fruit.

――――― COOK'S TIP ―――――

This compote will keep refrigerated for up to a week.

2 Remove the pan from the heat and stir in the raisins and honey. Cover the pan and leave to cool. Remove the cinnamon stick and then stir in the lemon juice.

3 Transfer the compote to a serving bowl, cover with clear film and keep refrigerated until needed. Allow the fruit compote to come to room temperature before serving, decorated with a few mint leaves.

Plum and Almond Tart

Plums and almonds have a natural affinity, and this Russian tart with its simple pastry case is a great way to serve them. Serve with home-made custard.

INGREDIENTS

Serves 6
175g/6oz/1½ cups plain flour
115g/4oz/8 tbsp butter, chilled
60ml/4 tbsp soured cream

For the topping
50g/2oz/4 tbsp butter, softened
50g/2oz/¼ cup caster sugar, plus
    30ml/2 tbsp for sprinkling
2 eggs, beaten
115g/4oz/1 cup ground almonds
about 6 plums, quartered and stoned
115g/4oz/scant ½ cup plum jam
60ml/4 tbsp flaked almonds

1 Sift the flour into a mixing bowl. Dice the butter and rub in until the mixture resembles fine breadcrumbs. Stir in the soured cream to make a soft dough. Wrap in clear film and chill for at least 30 minutes.

COOK'S TIP

Apricots can be used instead of plums, as an alternative, if liked.

---

2 For the topping, cream the butter and sugar until light. Add the eggs, alternating with the ground almonds.

3 Preheat the oven to 220°C/425°F/ Gas 7. Roll out the pastry on a lightly floured surface to a 30cm/12in round, then transfer to a large baking sheet. Prick all over.

4 Spread the almond mixture over the pastry, leaving a border of about 4cm/1½in. Arrange the plums on top. Sprinkle with the 30ml/2 tbsp caster sugar. Turn in the border.

5 Bake the tart for 35–40 minutes, or until browned. Warm the plum jam in a small pan, press through a sieve and brush over the tart to glaze. Sprinkle flaked almonds on top to decorate.

VARIATION

The recipe could be used to make 4 individual tarts, like the one shown here. Thickly slice the plums instead of cutting them into quarters. Finish the tarts as above with the jam glaze and flaked almonds.

Lepeshki

With characteristic Russian preference for all things sour, these biscuits are shortened with soured cream instead of butter.

INGREDIENTS

Makes 24
225g/8oz/2 cups self-raising flour
pinch of salt
90g/3½oz/½ cup caster sugar
1 egg, separated
120ml/4fl oz/½ cup soured cream
2.5ml/½ tsp each vanilla and
   almond essence
15ml/1 tbsp milk
50g/2oz/½ cup flaked almonds

1 Preheat the oven to 200°C/400°F/ Gas 6. Sift the flour, salt and sugar into a mixing bowl and make a well in the centre.

2 Reserve 10ml/2 tsp of the egg white. Mix the remainder with the egg yolk, soured cream, vanilla and almond essences and milk. Add to the dry ingredients and mix to form a soft dough.

3 Roll out the dough on a lightly floured surface until about 8mm/⅓in thick, then stamp out rounds with a 7.5cm/3in cutter.

4 Transfer the circles to lightly oiled baking sheets. Brush with the reserved egg white and sprinkle with the flaked almonds.

5 Bake for 10 minutes, until light golden brown. Transfer to a wire rack and allow to cool. Store the biscuits in an airtight container.

Pyrizhky

These delicious Russian turnovers comprise a double helping of nuts: a buttery almond pastry with a walnut and rum filling.

INGREDIENTS

Makes 12

150g/5oz/1¼ cups plain flour
pinch of salt
65g/2½oz/5 tbsp caster sugar
50g/2oz/½ cup ground almonds
90g/3½oz/7 tbsp butter, cubed
2.5ml/½ tsp vanilla essence
1 egg, beaten, plus extra for sealing
  and glazing

For the filling

25g/1oz/2 tbsp unsalted butter,
  softened
50g/2oz/½ cup icing sugar, sifted
1 egg yolk
50g/2oz/½ cup walnuts, finely
  chopped
10ml/2 tsp rum

1 Sift the flour, salt and 40g/1½oz/ 3 tbsp caster sugar into a bowl. Stir in the ground almonds. Rub in the butter until the mixture resembles fine breadcrumbs. Make a well in the centre.

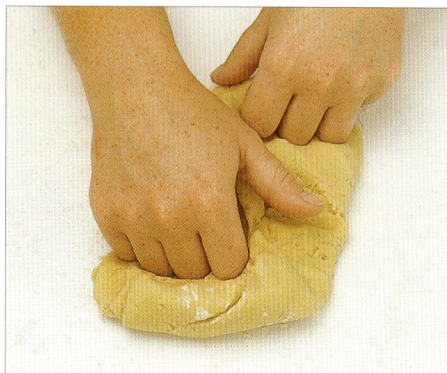

2 Add the vanilla essence and 1 beaten egg. Mix to a soft dough, then knead on a lightly floured surface for a few seconds until smooth. Wrap the dough in clear film and refrigerate for 40 minutes.

3 Meanwhile, for the filling, beat the butter and icing sugar together. Add the egg yolk and mix well. Fold in the walnuts and then stir in the rum.

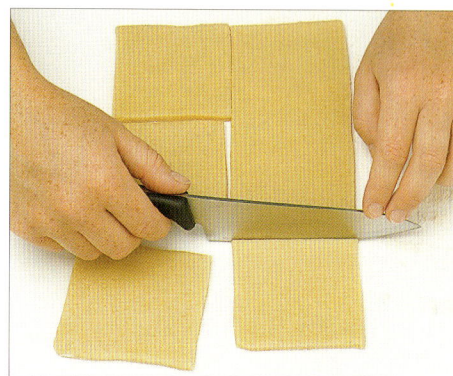

4 Preheat the oven to 200°C/400°F/ Gas 6. Roll out the pastry 3mm/ ⅛in thick on a lightly floured surface. Cut into 7.5cm/3in squares, using a sharp knife or a pastry wheel.

5 Brush the edges with beaten egg. Then place a spoonful of filling near one corner of each square.

6 Fold over the pastry to make triangles, then press the edges with a fork to seal. On a baking sheet, glaze with more egg and sprinkle with the remaining sugar. Bake for 15 minutes, until golden. Cool on a wire rack.

Babka

A typical Polish Easter menu is a grand affair and may include roast sucking pig, brightly coloured eggs and *Babka* – the word means "Grandmother". The cake was so named because it is made with gentleness and loving care.

INGREDIENTS

Serves 8
350g/12oz/3 cups plain flour
2.5ml/½ tsp salt
25g/1oz/2 tbsp caster sugar
5ml/1 tsp easy-blend dried yeast
115g/4oz/8 tbsp butter, softened
150ml/¼ pint/⅔ cup warm milk
4 egg yolks
115g/4oz/scant 1 cup sultanas
finely grated rind of 1 orange
60ml/4 tbsp clear honey, warmed
butter, to serve

1 Sift the flour, salt and sugar into a large bowl. Stir in the yeast, then make a well in the centre.

2 Add the butter, milk, egg yolks, dried fruit and orange rind. Mix to a dough. Turn out on a lightly floured surface and knead for 10 minutes, until smooth and elastic.

3 Put the dough in a well-greased 1.25kg/2½lb fluted cake tin. Cover with oiled clear film and leave in a warm place to rise for 1 hour, or until doubled in size.

4 Preheat the oven to 190°C/375°F/ Gas 5. Bake for 45–50 minutes, or until firm and a skewer inserted into the middle comes out clean.

5 Allow the cake to cool in the tin for 5 minutes. Turn out on to a wire rack and brush all over with the warmed honey. When cold, slice thickly and serve with butter.

Christmas Cookies

These spiced biscuits may be used as edible decorations: thread them with coloured ribbon and hang on the branches of the Christmas tree, as is traditionally done in the Ukraine.

INGREDIENTS

Makes 30
50g/2oz/4 tbsp butter
15ml/1 tbsp golden syrup or
   clear honey
50g/2oz/¼ cup soft light brown sugar
225g/8oz/2 cups plain flour
10ml/2 tsp ground cinnamon
5ml/1 tsp ground ginger
1.5ml/¼ tsp grated nutmeg
2.5ml/½ tsp bicarbonate of soda
45ml/3 tbsp milk
1 egg yolk
30ml/2 tbsp sugar crystals

1 Preheat the oven to 180°C/350°F/ Gas 4. Line 2 baking sheets with baking parchment. Melt the butter, syrup or honey and brown sugar in a pan. Leave to cool for 5 minutes.

2 Sift the flour, cinnamon, ginger, nutmeg and bicarbonate of soda into a bowl. Make a well in the centre. Pour in the melted butter mixture, milk and egg yolk. Mix to a soft dough.

3 Knead until smooth, then roll out between 2 sheets of baking parchment until 5mm/¼in thick. Stamp out rounds using biscuit cutters.

--- COOK'S TIP ---

Roll out the dough while it is still warm, since it becomes hard and brittle as it cools.

4 Place on the baking sheets. Make a hole in each with a skewer if you wish to hang them up later. Sprinkle with coloured sugar crystals. Bake for 10 minutes, until a slightly darker shade. Cool slightly, then transfer to a wire rack and leave to cool completely.

Sour Rye Bread

Traditionally, the "starter" would be a little dough left over from a previous bread-making session, but it's simple to make your own. The starter gives this bread its delicious, slightly sour taste.

INGREDIENTS

Makes 2 loaves

450g/1lb/4 cups rye flour, plus extra for dusting (optional)
450g/1lb/4 cups strong white flour
15ml/1 tbsp salt
7g/¼oz sachet easy-blend dried yeast
25g/1oz/2 tbsp butter, softened
600ml/1 pint/2½ cups warm water
15ml/1 tbsp caraway seeds or buckwheat, for sprinkling (optional)

For the sourdough starter
60ml/4 tbsp rye flour
45ml/3 tbsp warm milk

1 For the starter, mix the rye flour and milk together in a small bowl. Cover with clear film and leave in a warm place for 1–2 days, or until it smells pleasantly sour.

2 To make the loaves, sift together the flour and salt into a large bowl. Next stir in the yeast. Make a well in the centre and add the butter, water and sourdough starter already prepared. With a wooden spoon mix well until you have a soft dough.

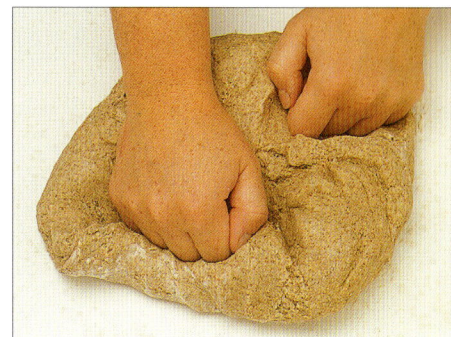

3 Turn out the dough on to a lightly floured surface and knead for 10 minutes, until smooth and elastic. Put in a clean bowl, cover with clear film and leave in a warm place to rise for 1 hour, or until doubled in size.

4 Knead for 1 minute, then divide the dough in half. Shape each piece into a round 15cm/6in across. Transfer to 2 greased baking sheets. Cover with oiled clear film and leave to rise for 30 minutes.

5 Preheat the oven to 200°C/400°F/ Gas 6. Brush the loaves with water, then sprinkle with caraway seeds or buckwheat, or dust with rye flour.

6 Bake for 35–40 minutes, or until the loaves are browned and sound hollow when tapped on the bottom. Cool on a wire rack.

COOK'S TIP

Sour rye bread keeps fresh for up to a week. This recipe can also be made without yeast, but it will be much denser.

Poppy Seed Roll

This sweet yeast bake with its spiral filling of dried fruits and poppy seeds is a wonderful example of traditional Polish cooking and is a firm favourite. The seeds have a gritty texture and keep the cake moist.

INGREDIENTS

Serves 12
450g/1lb/4 cups plain flour
pinch of salt
30ml/2 tbsp caster sugar
10ml/2 tsp easy-blend dried yeast
175ml/6fl oz/³⁄₄ cup milk
finely grated rind of 1 lemon
50g/2oz/4 tbsp butter

For the filling and glaze
50g/2oz/4 tbsp butter
115g/4oz/²⁄₃ cup poppy seeds
50ml/2fl oz/¹⁄₄ cup set honey
65g/2¹⁄₂ oz/¹⁄₂ cup raisins
65g/2¹⁄₂ oz/scant ¹⁄₂ cup finely
   chopped candied orange peel
50g/2oz/¹⁄₂ cup ground almonds
1 egg yolk
50g/2oz/¹⁄₄ cup caster sugar
15ml/1 tbsp milk
60ml/4 tbsp apricot jam
15ml/1 tbsp lemon juice
15ml/1 tbsp rum or brandy
25g/1oz/¹⁄₄ cup toasted
   flaked almonds

1 Sift the flour, salt and sugar into a bowl. Stir in the easy-blend dried yeast. Make a well in the centre.

2 Heat the milk and lemon rind in a pan with the butter, until melted. Cool a little, then add to the dry ingredients and mix to a dough.

3 Knead the dough on a lightly floured surface for 10 minutes, until smooth and elastic. Put in a clean bowl, cover and leave in a warm place to rise for 45–50 minutes, or until doubled in size.

4 For the filling, melt the butter in a pan. Reserve 15ml/1 tbsp of poppy seeds, then process the rest and add to the pan with the honey, raisins and peel. Cook gently for 5 minutes. Stir in the almonds; leave to cool.

5 Whisk the egg yolk and sugar together in a bowl until pale, then fold into the poppy seed mixture. Roll out the dough on a lightly floured surface to a rectangle 30 × 35cm/ 12 × 14in. Spread the filling to within 2.5cm/1in of the edges.

6 Roll both ends towards the centre. Cover with oiled clear film and leave to rise for 30 minutes. Preheat the oven to 190°C/375°F/Gas 5.

7 Brush with the milk, then sprinkle with the reserved poppy seeds. Bake for 30 minutes, until golden brown.

8 Heat the jam and lemon juice gently until bubbling. Sieve, then stir in the rum or brandy. Brush over the roll while still warm and scatter the almonds on top.

Braided Bread

This Ukrainian bread, *Kolach*, is served at many religious and family feasts. It is now usually only braided, but originally would have been shaped into a *kolo* (circle) – hence its name.

INGREDIENTS

Makes 1 large loaf

350g/12oz/3 cups strong white flour
5ml/1 tsp salt
5ml/1 tsp caster sugar
7g/¼oz sachet easy-blend dried yeast
150ml/¼ pint/⅔ cup milk
40g/1½oz/3 tbsp butter
1 egg, beaten, plus extra for glazing
10ml/2 tsp poppy seeds

1 Sift the flour, salt and sugar into a large bowl. Stir in the easy-blend dried yeast. Make a well in the centre.

2 In a pan, gently heat the milk with the butter until melted. Allow to cool until tepid, then add to the dry ingredients with the beaten egg. Mix to a soft dough.

3 Knead on a lightly floured surface for 10 minutes, or until smooth and elastic. Put in a clean bowl, cover with clear film and leave in a warm place to rise for 1 hour, or until doubled in size.

4 Preheat the oven to 200°C/400°F/ Gas 6. Turn out the dough on a lightly floured surface and knead for 1 minute until smooth. Divide into 3 equal pieces. Roll each into a "sausage" about 25cm/10in long.

5 Braid the 3 strands together, starting with an outside strand, and working your way down. Stick the ends under neatly at the end. Transfer to a lightly greased baking sheet. Cover with oiled clear film and leave to rise for 30 minutes.

6 Brush the loaf with beaten egg and sprinkle with the poppy seeds. Bake for 40–45 minutes or until golden brown. Cool on a wire rack.

Buckwheat Bread Rolls

These nutty-flavoured rolls are made using a mixture of flours, since buckwheat alone does not contain the gluten necessary for the bread to rise.

INGREDIENTS

Makes 16

350g/12oz/3 cups buckwheat flour
350g/12oz/3 cups strong white flour
10ml/2 tsp salt
7g/¼oz sachet easy-blend dried yeast
25g/1oz/2 tbsp butter, melted
about 600ml/1 pint/2½ cups
     warm water
30ml/2 tbsp olive oil
coarse salt, for sprinkling

1 Sift the flours and salt into a large bowl. Stir in the yeast and make a well in the centre. Add the butter and enough of the warm water to mix everything to a soft dough.

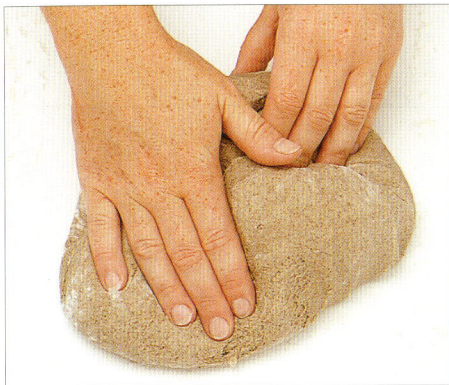

2 Knead the dough on a lightly floured surface for 10 minutes, or until smooth and elastic. Put in a clean bowl, cover with clear film and leave in a warm place to rise for 1 hour.

> ——— COOK'S TIPS ———
>
> Buckwheat is a member of the rhubarb family and has triangular seeds, which produce a sweet and speckled flour.

3 Lightly knead the dough again until smooth. Divide into 16 equal pieces. Roll each into a ball and put on a greased baking sheet, leaving plenty of space between them.

4 Cover the rolls with oiled clear film and leave to rise for 30 minutes. Meanwhile, preheat the oven to 200°C/400°F/Gas 6.

5 Brush the rolls with the olive oil and sprinkle lightly with the salt.

6 Bake for 25–30 minutes, or until well risen and lightly browned. Cool on a wire rack, covering with a dish towel to keep the crust soft.

INDEX